VICTIM OF CIRCUMSTANCES

Victim Of Circumstances

A memoir
by

RITA BAKER and
MARGOT SWICARCIK

Adelaide Books
New York / Lisbon
2019

VICTIM OF CIRCUMSTANCES
A memoir
By Rita Baker and Margot Swicarcik

Copyright © by Rita Baker and Margot Swicarcik
Cover design © 2019 Adelaide Books

Published by Adelaide Books, New York / Lisbon
adelaidebooks.org

Editor-in-Chief
Stevan V. Nikolic

All rights reserved. No part of this book may be reproduced in any manner whatsoever without written permission from the author except in the case of brief quotations embodied in critical articles and reviews.

For any information, please address Adelaide Books
at info@adelaidebooks.org
or write to:
Adelaide Books
244 Fifth Ave. Suite D27
New York, NY, 10001

ISBN:978-1-951896-07-2

Printed in the United States of America

For my daughter Ruth and granddaughter, Elana.

Contents

Forward. *9*

Simon. *11*

Margot. *37*

David. *137*

About Margot Swicarcik *161*

About Rita Baker *163*

Forward.

Hitler did not come out of a vacuum; he was the product of 2,000 years of ill will, towards the Jews, that began with the expulsion of the Jewish people from their homeland, by the Romans who presided over Israel at the time, putting 125,000 Israelites to death on the cross, Jesus being one of them, for fighting the Romans, in order to free their people from bondage.

Hitler came to power with 43.9% when President General Hindenburg, on the advice of the industrialist Krupp, gave the position of Chancellor to Hitler with the vote of the German people. Feeling that they had been stabbed in the back, the Communists in Berlin started to run around with red flowers in their lapels, shouting that the Social democrats had betrayed Germany.

Whilst this is a story depicting a shocking upheaval of the times, it is not the horrific story of a concentration camp survivor. It is the harrowing tale of one young girl's upbringing and whose courage, inner strength, and will to live through a time in history unparalleled by any other, was fostered by the extraordinary example of her beloved parents. It is the story of how she, Margot Davidowitch lived through personal tragedy in Hitler's Germany, and then in Poland and communist Russia, before, during and after W.W.11, coming out of that dark period, a complete person; a testament to that inner strength that remains with her to this day.

It is also the irrational tale of devastation and the hope that can come out of the ashes of war, and it gives the reader an insight into the life of a European Jewess, during that time. There is no question that fate played a large part in the lives of her family. When you read this biography, you will understand how and why.

Simon.

I lived through a time, in Europe, like no other time in the history of the Jewish People; one that not even the Spanish inquisition can compare with; and these are my stories.

Firstly, I will begin with my father, Simon, a man of vision who, but for him, I might not have survived; and so I will start at the beginning that will explain how my mother, Ruth, and my father and I came to be living in Germany at the time of that maniac, Hitler, and tell it as my father explained it to me.

It was well beyond the middle of the night, and my parents were in bed asleep, when suddenly, with a start, my father's eyes shot open; there was no mistaking the pounding sound of a dozen boots mounting the stairs in the building in which we lived and his heart sank. The morning light was still inching its way across the sky like a dark blanket, slowly, being rolled back. Waiting for its arrival always excited my father, a new day, a new beginning; but that morning, he wanted to weep.

The shocking and unrivalled things that were going on, in Germany, after Hitler came to power, were taking a toll on my father. Ordinary citizens, hard-working people who had lived in and loved their German homeland for hundreds of years, were being awakened in the early hours of the morning, taken from their beds by Hitler's agents of terror and brutally beaten and mutilated for no reason other than being born into the Jewish faith. Such madness was terrifying to the German Jews. To my father, not a native of Germany, even more so. He was born in Poland, and having read 'MEIN CAMPF', he realized that Hitler was crazy and that his desire was to wipe the Jewish people, not merely of Germany, but off the face of the entire European continent.

Suddenly, what he had feared most was upon us and, his brain numb with fear, my father nudged my mother, Ruth.

Half asleep, she turned to him, "What is it Simon?" asked my mother.

"They're on the stairs. They will soon be here!" replied my father.

Sitting bolt upright, my mother gasped "...You mean...?"

"Wake Margot, but don't frighten her. We have to think of something and quickly," he said.

Her bare feet ready to run, my mother whispered, "I'm scared, Simon."

Seconds later, she was knocking on her cousin Frauline Zelniger's door, the beautiful, blonde, dancer with the Straus Travelling Company, who happened to be spending that night with us, and quickly explained the situation "They have yet to reach us. Stay where you are," breathlessly, her cousin whispered, "I must get to the door before they have a chance to see your name. Quickly, go back to your husband and wait."

Barely able to breath, when my mother returned, my father grabbed her hand holding it tight. She glanced at him, her eyes wide with fear, and swallowed.

Without her usual glance in the mirror, Frauline Zelniger rushed to the door, and the moment she heard the first dreaded knock, threw the door wide open before the Gestapo had time to see a name and using all her skills as a performer, she leaned, seductively, against the door post, and with a flirtatious gleam in her eyes, asked "What are you doing waking good decent citizens at this hour of the morning?"

She was wearing nothing but a revealing pure silk night dress that, immediately, caught the eye of one of the Nazi officers and his lips twisted into a lecherous grin. "Had I known such a beautiful woman was living here, I would have called sooner," he said, his eyes wandering over her breasts, her hips, her thighs.

Appearing relaxed and confident, with a coquettish tilt of her head, my mother's cousin responded, "It's a good thing for you that my fiancé, a high ranking diplomat you might have heard of, is still at the German embassy in Paris, or he might've had something to say about this!"

The officer's mouth fell open, and feeling somewhat of a fool, he stammered "For...give me madam, I...I had no idea anyone important lived here." And with a click of his heels, he led his men away, shining their torch at door after door, searching for the name of a Jewish family to terrorize with their brutality.

Breathlessly, she entered my parent's bedroom and closing the door fell back against it with a sigh of relief. "... You're safe... for now," she whispered.

It took a while before my parents were able to come to themselves. They had just been saved by a woman's beauty and charm and thankful as they were, it was still a fearful moment for my father, and scared to death, he then and there decided they had to leave Germany.

By whose Grand Design does life dare to play its tricks on us poor unsuspecting human beings? By God's? By fate's? Are they not one and the same? How can there be a God, a ruler of the universe, without fate? Or fate without the hand of He who ordains all things in heaven and earth? And it is by such design that fate leads us to our final destination.

For centuries, Poland was a land partitioned between Russia, Austria and Prussia until around 1830 when the Polish people, rashly, engaged in a rebellion which only hastened their complete absorption into Russia.

In the year 1895, my father, Simon Davidowitch was born and, at the tender age of fourteen, he, together with his friend, Karl, joined a group of Polish freedom fighters, against the Czar; and so it was that fate took my father along that rocky road that leads all mankind to their destiny.

It was his youthful enthusiasm for the cause that soon caught the attention of the Russians. Having been warned of his impending capture and internment, My father, together with Karl, then made their escape to Denmark.

They found Copenhagen a warm friendly city, and there they remained for a number of years; yet as nice as it was, there was something missing for the two young men brimming with life; they needed more than what Denmark had to offer, and the city that called to them was Berlin; the city of Goethe and Heine and a culture unmatched anywhere else in Europe. An exciting city with its bright lights, theatres, beer halls and coffee houses, and, Oh! So alive.

During the reign of Kaiser Wilhelm 11, German industry boomed and the military became one of Europe's most efficient. However, the Kaiser's ambition was to create a naval power that would rival Great Britain's. But it didn't stop there, he wanted to form an empire that would bring about the fall of Britain's Supreme authority and it proved his undoing.

With the continuing European dissent, the Kaiser saw an opportunity to realize his aim and he was, whole heartedly, supported by the entire German nation, and to war he went with those thoughts in mind.

In the heavy fighting with the European nations to its west, and Russia to its east, Germany had taken on a massive task. Even so, they might have achieved their objective, if America hadn't come into the war in 1917, the same year as the Russian revolution took place and, with whose leaders Germany made a deal enabling them to withdraw its troops from Russian soil and place them on its Western front. Still, magnificently as they fought, they were no match in face of the numbers that fought against them.

It was in 1917, just before the Kaiser's treaty with Russia, that my father and his friend, Karl, entered Germany. Although they were still at war with Russia, having fought against the Russians themselves, my father and Karl believed they were safe. Not so, they were still considered Russian Nationals and would dearly pay the price if caught.

Now my father had a cousin, Mala, whom he believed was still living in Berlin and he set out to find her, coming to a dead end at every turn. It was frustrating, and he decided his only course was to go to the police and see what they could find out for him.

As yet, my father had no knowledge of the war regulations and his status in Germany, and the reaction of the captain in charge came as a shock when he mentioned the name of his cousin, who was known to be a communist and married to a Russian with whom she ran away to Moscow.

Realizing the impossible situation in which he had placed himself, my father did what he always did best, when faced with danger; he talked himself out of it, explaining how he himself fought against the Russian occupation of Poland, and telling stories of the fight, aware that with his commanding voice and impressive figure, he could hold an audience captive and the chief of police was no exception, hanging on every word that came from my father's lips.

When he finished, the officer gave thought for a moment. "I'll tell you what," he said, "find yourself a sponsor that will help get you a job, and you won't be interned. Now get out of here, and be quick before I change my mind."

My father didn't have to be told twice, and he hastened out of there as fast as his legs could carry him.

As it was, my father had left his friend, Karl, outside, when he went in, now he was nowhere to be seen and, frustrated, he threw up his arms in despair, and went in search of him, unfortunately, to no avail.

Karl, who found the waiting too long, worried about his friend and had ventured inside the police station in search of him when, unexpectedly, he was questioned and held as a Russian Nationalist and immediately interned. It wasn't until weeks later, that my father discovered what happened to him; meanwhile, he realized that his first priority was to find himself work if he was to remain out of harm's way.

With no one to turn to, my father's only option was to search the pages of a directory for something, anything, that gave hope, and that is where he found a name staring back at him; a physician called Levy, Doctor Levy, and he immediately made an appointment making certain that he would be the last patient to be seen by the doctor, giving my father enough time to explain his predicament.

Dr. Levy was a German through and through identifying himself with the German people before that of his Hebrew heritage so, when he questioned my father about the medical reason for his visit, only to be told that it had nothing to do with illness and that having nowhere else to turn, he had come, as one Jew to another, for advice on how to go about getting employment by someone who would be willing to sponsor him and thus avoid his being interned as a Russian Nationalist, the doctor saw red.

With eyes flaring in anger, he went into a rage, throwing his arms about, shouting and screaming at my father, accusing him of insulting him and being insensitive to his role as a good German doctor to the good German people whom he served.

To my father, that someone would take such a position was inconceivable, and with his own anger rising, he gave the doctor a piece of his mind. "Do you expect me to ask forgiveness for believing that one Jew would have the decency to help another?" he said. "Where I come from, a Jew would never turn another Jew away. That is how I was brought up, to always be there for those of my brethren in need"

The doctor, apoplectic with fury, snapped "Get out of my office!"

My father couldn't believe his ears; to be treated like that...! and fuming, he shook a finger at him. "No! "He shouted. "Not before you've heard me out, and you will hear me out," his commanding tone silencing the doctor. "I am not a criminal and I am not a Russian, I have nothing to do with the Russians. I come from the town of Lodz and I hate the Russians as much as you do and fought them, myself, on behalf of Poland. I recently came here from Copenhagen where I have been living. I had no idea, until I arrived, that I would be looked upon as a Russian Nationalist...! I have not come here to beg but to ask, as one decent human being to another. Now...! Do you know of anyone who might vouch for me and give me work that will keep me from being placed in an internment camp like a common thief?"

He'd hit a nerve and, somewhat shame-faced, the doctor calmed down and after giving it due thought, he said "...All right, I will introduce you to my brother who owns a coffee house. At the moment it has been taken over by the army as a club for high ranking officers but it's still run by my brother. That is as much as I can do without placing myself in difficulty, and not because you are Jewish, make no mistake about that, but because you appear to be an intelligent young man."

The doctor's brother was an affable fellow and, immediately, offered my father a job as a waiter in the restaurant. "Of course, we are at war with Russia and, you being a Russian National, I would have to clear it first with the officers, but If I vouch for you, I see no problem there," he said.

However grateful my father was, being a waiter wasn't quite what he had in mind; "I am clumsy," he said. "I would hate to spill some of your good coffee over a German officer's uniform."

The brother smiled. "I understand perfectly. I have a snooker hall upstairs; you could keep score, that is, if you're not too clumsy to hold a piece of chalk?"

And that is how my father managed to get a foot on the ladder to success.

The officers soon took to him; they loved listening to his stories, and as soon as he began to feel comfortable with them, he broached the subject of his friend, Karl, who had been placed in a one of their camps for foreign nationals. They were sympathetic, but could do nothing about it except to find out which camp he was in.

When my father saw him, he was horrified to see how much weight he had lost, and felt guilty about his situation. "Tell me?" curiously he asked through the barbed wire that separated them, "whatever possessed you to go looking for me inside the police station?"

"When you didn't come out, I was worried," he replied.

My father couldn't believe what he heard. "...Goylem!" he cried, "If you were so afraid, you should have run, not entered the lion's den."

"I don't understand; how come they put me in here and not you?" bewildered, he asked.

My father patted his lips. "... That's how, You have to know how to talk your way out!"

Although there was nothing my father could do to free Karl, his new found friends felt sorry about it when they heard of his deteriorating condition and allowed my father to take over food from the restaurant; and so Karl became the best fed internee, in the camp.

In the year 1918, Germany lost the war, bringing about the abdication of the Kaiser, which resulted in a federation of republics for Germany. Humiliation might have humbled a lesser people, but not so the staunch German population; to them it was simply a thorn in their side, one that would be removed once they got back on their feet. My father was no longer considered a Russian National and in that atmosphere, he found a place for himself at last, as did his friend, Karl, who was subsequently released.

My father, tall and good looking with fine brown, intelligent eyes and a wide expressive mouth, always had a hankering for the stage and turned to amateur dramatics, and with his artistic temperament and powerful voice he was well suited to the life of an actor. It also taught him the art of projecting himself, which was to come in good stead for the future troubles that would afflict Germany.

Later, my father believed that it would be to his advantage to meet other bright young people who were as interested in politics as he was, and he joined the Social Democratic Party where he met Herman Bucholtz, a man of equal intelligence with whom he would enjoy an unshakeable and close friendship.

Opportunity rarely knocks on a person's door, but when it does, it takes a wise man to seize the moment, and my father was that wise man.

His friend, Bucholtz, tall, blond and handsome, was the chief designer for a textile factory. One day, he mentioned to my father that the owner of the factory had brought his daughter round and introduced her to him. Having become acquainted with the class structure of German society, my father knew that in no way would a member of the upper class mix socially with a person of a lower sphere. So what was the story there? wondered my father. Could it be, that having no sons of his own, the mill owner wanted to secure the future of his only daughter and saw Bucholtz as a man that was, not only, a superb designer but also one who understood the working of a mill, such as his, and what was needed to maintain its position as one of Germany's top textile factories.

"Didn't you find it strange that the owner of the mill would do such a thing?" asked my father.

"Of course! But then who knows why some people do what they do?" With a shrug said Bucholtz.

With a quizzical lift of his brow my father said, "I think I do! He brought her along to take a look at you," and with a smile, slapped Herman on the back.

Bucholtz chuckled. "You're out of you mind!"

"Think so! Tell me, what did you think of her?" asked my father.

"She's easy to look at, that's for sure. She is also bright and has a pleasant manner."

"Bet she thought the same about you!" said my father.

Bucholtz gave him a friendly poke in the stomach. "You really do have some absurd ideas, you know!"

"We'll see!" smiled my father with a friendly poke back.

Two weeks later, Bucholtz told my father that he had been invited to Christmas dinner at the home of the mill owner.

"You are going, of course," he said to Bucholtz.

"I can hardly refuse, he's my boss; but then, if it's a union between his daughter and me, that he's looking for, I have no intention of marrying her or anyone else. I haven't lived enough yet, and I don't want to be bogged down by a wife, especially the boss's daughter."

"I thought you found her pleasing?" Said my father.

"So?"

"So don't be a fool, Bucholtz! Now listen to me;" said my father. "you will go to that dinner party and be as charming as only you know how, and what is more, you will marry the girl and become an important member of the family."

"I don't understand; what is it to you?"

"I'll tell you what it is to me," replied my father. "One day you will become the president of one of the most prestigious companies in Germany; and when you do, I want to be your representative for the entire city of Berlin."

His friend grinned, "She's still not my type."

"You'll get used to her. Besides, from what you told me she is well educated and charming; so why would you want to remain a textile designer forever, if you can become an influential person with a good life as the owner of a huge company?" said my father.

"I see your point!"

And so my father got his way, and when his friend became the president of the corporation, he made him his representative, and he together with my father, became a force to be reckoned with in the world of business.

Time! A clock ticking; a world changing; and as the clock ticked, Germany was changing. The nineteen fourteen, eighteen war was long over, and the Fatherland was suffering, and when people suffer, they look for someone, anyone to lead them out of their misery. The twenties were volatile; my father could feel the change coming; but life was too good for him to concern himself with it. Perhaps it was the young lady, my mother, that he met who changed his life. For the first time, he realized what an empty shell he was without the right woman by his side, and that young lady, bright, attractive with magnificent green eyes, silky, long, black hair and an inviting figure, was not only warm and good natured, but intelligent, well educated and well read with a commanding presence that would make people sit up and take notice the moment she entered a room. As well, my mother was a very able woman who could sow or keep books; whatever she put a hand to she could do and do well. In short, she had all the qualities a man could wish for in a wife and more. So, at the late age of thirty eight, my father married; and four years later I was born, and as my parents told me, a bright, gifted child inheriting my father's love of storytelling, and with a voice that matched his with its clarity and resonance, as well as my mother's, lovely, green eyes.

Apart from that niggle, at the back of his mind, that kept reminding my father of the uncertain times we were living in, life could not have been more perfect for the three of us. It was in that world of complete comfort and security that I, an only child, that was doted on by my parents, grew up. Even at the age of six, I showed an intelligence beyond my years, encouraged by my parents who treated me as an adult, always with an explanation when the answer was 'no' to something I wanted that they considered inappropriate, giving me an insight into the way we lived our lives. Yet, still, I managed to remain a child with all the love a child has in them, and I was loved by one and all, whether Jewish or Christian, it made no difference to a German, in those days, when anti-Semitism was never an issue; so, as a lively child, I was always popular, smiling and happy, and full of the joys of youth.

I went to a Catholic public school and was in the first grade with children of all denominations. That I was of the Jewish faith while others were not, never entered my head; I was simply, one of them, until one day, a religious teacher came into the school room and asked the mistress how many Jewish children were in her class, "I am certain there must be quite a few of them, the school being in a predominately Jewish district," he said

"I know nothing about that," she replied, "why don't you ask them?"

So he said, "Will all those that are Jewish, please come forward."

I was the only one that stood up and said, "I am Jewish."

The religious teacher appeared confused. "That is impossible," he said. "I am going to the principal's office to ask him."

"Don't go to the principal, he knows nothing about how many Jewish children are in the school; we don't keep the papers here. You will have to go to the City Hall," said the class mistress.

Two weeks later, he came again. He now knew that there were eight Jewish children in the class, and when these children heard this, they began crying. "Please, please, we don't want to leave Miss Weber's class to go with you."

As young as I was, I became impatient with them and said, "Don't be foolish, it's only religion and we are Jews, and we have this religion and Mr. Cytrin is the teacher of religion."

Mr. Cytrin's face broadened into a smile and he joked, "You, curly head, how comes you are so smart?"

"Because my father, he is from Lodz and he has family there that are very, very religious, and when I visit them, I know, from them, that I am a Jewess."

"Then tell your father that your religious teacher is also from Lodz."

And so I went through my early childhood, content and happy, unaware of what was in store for me and my family; and what was in store, was more terrifying than anything anyone could possibly imagine.

In the early thirties, Hitler came to power on the promise of better times for the German people. Almost immediately, stories circulated as to how the Gestapo were invading the homes of communists, gypsies and Jewish people, and behaving with such cruelty towards them, even mutilating them. Here were stories that no one wanted to believe, most of all the Jewish people, who had always thought of themselves as German first and foremost.

"He is only concerned with the Jews in Eastern Europe," they would whisper amongst themselves, "we have nothing to fear; we are German!"

Nevertheless, it was worrying; and often, in the early morning, my parents would awaken me and I would go out into the street to see what was happening and report back to them.

It wasn't a dangerous practice; as yet, they weren't touching women or young girls; anyhow, I was a feisty youngster who was only too happy that my parents trusted me enough to give me such an important mission, one that made me feel useful.

A strange thing happened, when I was out, one morning. There was a local store called, 'Levy', so it was only natural to assume that the owner was of the Hebrew faith. Not so! The name must have been in the family for generations when a Jew named Levy married into a Christian household and the name was retained.

Whether the man was stupid or not, he never gave it a thought, he was a Christian, and that was as much as he knew. When the thugs came and threw a brick threw his window, and then pulled the, protesting, gentleman out onto the street and began hitting him, he continued to protest, and the more he protested, the harder they hit him. "With a name like Levy, you are not a Jew!" they laughed, and hit him even harder.

Horrified by what I saw I ran home to tell my parents what had taken place.

They were aghast. It was a name, only a name and the man might have paid with his life because of a name.

How people fool themselves when it suits them. Not even the atrocities that were going on, the plundering of people's homes, made the right impact upon the good, Jewish, citizens of Hitler's Germany. They still believed it would come to nothing and that, before long, all would return to what it was.

Return to what it was! How could it? Wondered my father who, himself, had witnessed the vilest atrocity while walking home, one evening, with a cousin who was staying with us. Hitler surrounded himself with an army of young, arm band wearing, thugs who had the authority to go out into the streets and commit unspeakable acts against the Jewish people. On the day that my father and his cousin saw them, they were attacking a religious Jewish man, with a long beard, who was on his way home, and getting hold of this defenceless gentleman, they cut off his beard, taking a good part of the chin along with it, all the while laughing and kicking him, finding it amusing. Shaken and sick to their stomach, my father and his cousin, who was trembling with fear, returned home and, while they related the story to me and my mother, we were dumbstruck with horror, and the young cousin began breaking out in a sweat. That evening, he went to bed with a high temperature, and next day, just as soon as he recovered sufficiently, he left Berlin to return to his home in Lodz, Poland.

We the Davidowich family lived in an apartment building and were one of the only three Jewish families living there whilst the others were mainly of the Christian faith. In the early days, before Hitler, there was no antisemitism there was no anti-Semitism, and the Jews and the gentiles would live together in harmony. There was, however, a communist living in the building, a Herr Kranz. In Hitler's Germany, communists were seen as a threat to the nation, placing them on a par with the Jews.

Herr Kranz, was a pleasant young man who always had a smile and a 'good morning' for my father.

Suddenly, my father realized that he hadn't been seen for some time - He had been picked up by the Gestapo and placed in a detention camp for undesirables.

Three months went by when he suddenly appeared again. He was a changed man, and never acknowledged my father again.

Wondering about it, my father approached him, one morning, and asked, "What is it? Herr Kranz? Have I offended you in some way?"

Sheepishly, he looked down, whispering, "You haven't offended me, I am ashamed to look you straight in the face."

"But why?" asked my father.

"Because I am a Nazi," he replied. "You see, I have always wanted what was best for my people, and thought that it could be achieved through communism; but whilst I was in the camp, they re-educated me and I realized that what Hitler wants for us, is the same as what I want for the German people, for everyone to live well. Hitler is doing so much for us; he is building the Autobahn and everyone will own a car and there will be prosperity for all the German people. So you see, that is why I am now a Nazi."

My father couldn't believe what he heard. "Tell me," he asked, "Do you believe that when Moses brought his people out of bondage, and to feed them, God sent down manna from heaven?"

Somewhat taken aback, he answers, "No, of course not!"

"Then how do you think Hitler can make it happen, unless he has the backing of all the top industrialists of the Western world behind him? And for that, you will have to pay with your blood on the Russian front, because that is what they want Hitler to do, destroy communist Russia. I, personally, wouldn't mind if communist Russia disappeared, but the price of this will be World War 11, and that will cause a big upheaval for the whole of Europe," said my father.

"I see what you mean; but, Herr Davidowitch, understand that I am not of your faith and not as clever as you are. Your people have lived through two thousand years of hardship, and that has made you very wise; anyhow, now it is too late, I want to live. But I must tell you this; they will make shit of you, so you should leave Germany as soon as possible."

My father had already decided on leaving, and Herr Kranz only confirmed what he knew would be the right thing to do and thus we came to that fateful night, when we were saved by a cousin, a woman who put herself in danger, to save her family.

Later, that same night, my father said to my mother, "I don't think we can stay here any longer; e were lucky once; I can't see us being lucky twice. I'm a Polish citizen, therefore, as much as I hate to go back, we need to go to Poland because there is no other option for us... I will phone Bucholtz first thing in the morning."

All at once reminiscent, for the first time in months, my father smiled to himself, "Did I tell you that way back in those early days of our friendship, Hermann saved me from drowning?" he said to my mother. He was a great swimmer and from a high cliff, he dived into a river like a champion; and like a fool, I followed and would have drowned but for him. Strange how a sinking man will continue to struggle when help arrives, and that's how it was with me; I fought him like a man half crazed out of his mind; but did it deter him? Not him; grabbing a handful of my hair and, with my arms still flailing about, he dragged me to safety…I know Bucholtz! He'll do whatever is necessary to help us."

First thing, next day, my father telephoned him. "I need you urgently, Hermann, come over immediately," he said.

Bucholtz asked no questions, it was enough that his dear friend needed him, And getting into his car, he drove 60 miles from his estate to Berlin, and our apartment.

"So what is it that's so urgent…?" he asked.

Sadly, my father stared at his friend. "…They came here in the early hours of the morning, Hitler's thugs, and if it were not for Frauline Zelniger our cousin, I have no idea what might have happened to us. We need to leave Germany, and as quickly as possible."

Bucholtz gave a hopeless sigh. "… This can't last; in the meantime, you must bring your family to my home; you will stay there, on my estate, until this madness ends. You will be safe with us."

My father shook his head…. "You are wrong, Bucholtz; there will be war, and for us to wait until the last minute would be suicide."

"You're making too much of it; the people won't stand for Hitler for long," he argued.

"What is it with you, Bucholtz? Have you been such a 'fat cat' for so long that you no longer understand politics? This is about communism and the world needs a buffer against Stalin and what he stands for, and they see Hitler as the man to do what is needed," cried my father.

"I still think you are reading too much into it. Communism will never gain ground in Western Europe," said Bucholtz.

"You don't think so! Did you know there are six million well organized communists in Germany who are connected to

Moscow, dangerously so; and another four million in France? It frightens Europe and America; and that is why the industrialists of England, France and the United States, together with Krupp and Siemen's, are behind Hitler. They want him to go to war with Russia, therefore he must attack Poland in order to get through to her, and it won't stop there, my friend, Hitler is too ambitious; so who will be next?" asked my father.

"Are you saying it will be the First World War all over again? It would be madness," said Bucholtz.

"That's right! And what is more, the time will come when you will have to wear Hitler's uniform, not that you will want to, but to survive."

Bucholtz cringed, "Never!"

"Never...! They will expect a man in your position to be a good example to the people and it will work to your advantage unless you want to die... So what will it be? Live or die?"

It was then that Bucholtz understood what my father was telling him, and with a gasp he cried, "My God! You are right, I see that now. I don't know where my mind has been... Of course I want to live, and of course you must get away and as soon as possible."

"We must leave for Poland. But I'm afraid for my wife and daughter; what with the Gestapo hooligans everywhere, always searching and searching for Jews to kick and beat and torture, it's dangerous to travel, especially by train. They board at every stop, looking for us. We need your help if we are to get away unharmed. You must also help us with our money. We dare not withdraw it ourselves. We do not want to alert anyone."

"I understand what you're saying..." and after a moment's thought Bucholtz said, "I shall be there at the train station with you; but there must be no connection between us. I shall make certain to take the next carriage to yours, and should I hear any trouble, I shall immediately put a stop to it. And you are right, you will need money when you reach Poland. As you said, you cannot' withdraw any from the bank yourself or it might alert them. I will attend to that; all I need is the account number; I know people that I can trust in the banking world and will see that the funds are there waiting for you when you reach your destination. I'll give you the name of the bank later when I telephone with further instructions. In the meantime, take only the bare essentials with you; no photographs, understand? You mustn't arouse anyone's suspicion, especially if you're searched... And see to it that you take the first train tomorrow, after nightfall."

My father sighed with relief. "Thank you..." he said. "Whatever happens in the future, I shall never forget this"

"The future! How we looked forward to the future when we were young – remember Simon, those early years of naive trust?"

"I remember!" wistfully, said my father.

Suddenly their arms were about one another, friends, perhaps for the last time in their lives.

"Well?" asked my mother, when Bucholtz had left.

"Be ready to leave for the railway station tomorrow evening. Pack nothing but overnight clothes; we don't want anyone to suspect that we are leaving for good; if anyone should ask, we are visiting friends in the country," explained my father.

"Photos? I can't leave photos behind, I don't want to forget anything," said my mother, tears stinging her eyes.

"What was good, we will remember. For now, our safety is at stake. What is important is Margot and, thank god, she will be with us."

"I'll be ready," agreed my mother.

An hour later, my father heard from Bucholtz with the name of the bank. "I'll be at the station before you tomorrow," he said "and remember, you must not arrive before dark. I shall be in the next carriage to yours, that way I will be close at hand should there be any trouble, and whatever happens, or whatever I have to do to protect you, you don't know me."

No sooner had he replaced the receiver, than my father was deep in thought. "... You know what, I must warn our friend Maurice... Margot, come down with me; we must persuade him to leave with us." he said.

Maurice had a clothing store at street level at the front of the apartment building; he was busy with a customer when my father and I arrived, and upon seeing us, he beckoned his manager to take his place at the counter. "I've never seen you looking so tense before," said Maurice, "What is it? What's happened?"

"Not here, let's go into your office, we need to talk privately," whispered my father.

Maurice's office, which was at the back of the store, was small and apart from a steel filing cabinet, there was a mahogany desk that occupied half the space and a few leather chairs the rest. "Well?" he asked when they were seated.

"There was an incident, last night, that frightened the life out of me," and my father then explained what took place. "... We are leaving for Poland tomorrow evening for good. I have just heard from Bucholtz. He will be accompanying us as far as the border should something happen and we need him to help us. You must come with us; you do understand why?"

"It's true that I have been worrying about the situation, but tomorrow evening? What about the store? I can't leave it just like that. It's alright for you, your money is in cash; my money is all tied up in this," he said with a sweep of his hand.

Exasperated with him, my father said, "... You don't understand, you have nothing, Maurice."

"What are you talking about? You know how much this store is worth?" he cried.

"I know what it's worth to you, not one single mark; but to your manager, that is another matter. I've noticed the way he looks at you; it's only a matter of time before he gives you up to the Gestapo, and all this, that you believe is yours, will be his."

Maurice's brow knit and my father, realizing what a tough decision it was for someone who had put a life's time work into making a success of a business, waited, if somewhat impatiently, for his response... suddenly, Maurice asked, "So what must I do, Simon?"

"Call your wife, we need to explain the situation to her. If she agrees, then you have to be ready to leave tomorrow evening; and remember, she must pack only the bare essentials. Don't forget to leave the front door unlocked as though you will be returning shortly... One more thing, do not tell the children what is going on; you don't want them mentioning it to anyone else."

"So how come you are talking in front of your daughter?" he complained.

"She has a grown-up head on her shoulders and understands the situation as well as I do."

Stroking his chin in thought for a moment, Maurice called his wife, who was at the back of the store, and they explained the situation to her... It didn't take much convincing before she readily agreed to leave the next evening.

"Good!" With a sigh of relief my father declare. "Bucholtz will be at the station when we get there; but remember, we do not know him and he does not know us. It will be alright, he will attend to anything untoward that might happen before or whilst we are on the train. They will take notice of him, he is well known in high circles."

They arrived at the station fifteen minutes before the train was due to depart. Bucholtz was there, as promised, wearing an arm band with a Swastika; my father would never have believed, had you told him, that one day he would be thankful to see one on his friends arm and know that if anything, should it come to it, it would be their saviour.

They chose a carriage, and were about to board when it was as if all hell had broken loose. Somehow, Maurice's son, Daniel, had figured out that they were going to Poland and, remembering the last time they paid a visit to his father's family, to everyone's horror, he began screaming. "... I'm not going there, you can't take me; they don't have proper lavatories, they're in the back yard and they're dirty and dark and smelly. I'm not going, I'm not!" and, still screaming, he tried to tug away from his mother, who was trying to pull him onto the train.

Watching in dismay, my father was beside himself, all the plans Bucholtz had made might now be in jeopardy. He glanced at him out of the corner of his eye; Bucholtz was looking around, trying to appear casual; it didn`t fool my father who knew that he must have been feeling as sick at heart as he was when, suddenly, to everyone's relief, Maurice clapped a hand over the child's mouth and lifting him up, literally, shoved him into one of the compartments.

Whilst the train chugged along the tracks, my mother, Ruth, stared from the window into the darkness, remembering, with a pang, the Berlin that she had grown up in and loved with its vibrancy and excitement; the Cabaret's where sensuous performers, such as Marlene Dietrich, began their career and, of course, the burlesque humour that, sometimes, bordered on the indecent; it was brash, bawdy and good fun! The coffee houses where people went to see and be seen; the women, wearing fashionable little hats, sitting beside their husbands, discussing the latest news and its effect on their way of life. The theatres, the concerts, the walks on a week-end with everyone smartly dressed strolling along Unter Den Linden whilst music poured out of the cafes into the street. The beach at Wannsee where the Berliners would take their families to soak up the summer sun. The political rallies that she and my father enjoyed so much, where guest speakers would put forward their particular views and principles and the round of stimulating discussions that followed; how alive it made them feel, how necessary, it was, to their existence. Then there were the balls where they danced the night away. … A smile suddenly raised the corners of my mother's mouth when she recalled my telling them that I, too, wanted to go to a ball, that evening. "You are going to a ball, it's called the feather ball," she said as she tucked the billowing goose down comforter up under my chin and kissed me goodnight. … Berlin, after dark, was breathlessly aglitter as if someone had waved a magic wand and bathed the city in an incandescent light, drawing the people from their homes ready to taste the glamorous temptations of one of the world's great cities and magical it was, especially to my mother who loved everything about Berlin; my mother was well suited to city life and couldn't imagine living any other way … How enchanting it had been… How surreal… What was in store for them now? swallowing, she wondered.

She turned to my father, who had been watching her, and sighed. Understanding, he took her hand in his.

Margot.

'War for the sake of peace'! What kind of peace does war achieve? War is waged to conquer not to make peace. Neither is peace for the victor when the losers will always bide their time to take revenge. It is a matter of the heart being ruled by the mind. Unfortunately, the mind, in the case for war, is never ruled by a heart that longs for peace. The beast in man always prevails, making war, down through the ages, inevitable.

When we reached Poland, we settled in the new city of Gdynia on the Baltic coast, built by the Polish so that they could have their own harbour. Although they were allowed, by law, to use the port of Gdansk, the Germans, who were in control of the city, denied them their legal right.

As soon as we were settled in, they sent me to the only school available which was a Catholic school. There were but a few Jews living in the city, therefore there was no need of any others and I, being of an open mind, attempted to fit in.

Each morning, before lessons began, the children would stand up, say their prayers and then cross themselves. The girl sitting next to me noticed that I didn't do the same and surprised by the omission, asked with curiosity, "why don't you cross yourself?"

Thinking nothing foreboding about the question, I answered immediately. "Because I'm Jewish."

It was as though the girl had been struck by lightning, and with her eyes wide in fear she gasped, "I'm not sitting next to any dirty Jew," and moved away.

During the recess, she made certain that every other child in the class knew that there was a Jew amongst them.

Often, it is difficult to comprehend the behaviour of the human race. The evil intent towards others because of their differences be it religious or otherwise. What is certain is that those who can soften these attitudes, such as the schools and houses of worship, fail to do so.

Who can say what went through the minds of my class mates, but when they saw me, they came at me with such viciousness, almost tearing the clothes on my back as if I was some kind of wild animal running amok amongst them, when all along, it was they who were acting like the beasts in the forests of humanity.

Scared and shocked by what was happening, I looked to the teacher for help;, but all she did was look the other way, obviously condoning the actions of her pupils.

When my mother saw the condition in which I returned home, the very next day, she went to see the principal. "For years, my daughter went to school, in Hitler's Germany, and nothing like this ever happened. How come you allow it to happen here?" she asked in anger.

The principal's eyes glinted with spite. "Listen," he said "if you people of the Old Testament want to live here, I can do nothing about it.... But- let-us-have- one-city- without- a- Jew- in- it," he emphasised with more than a hint of repugnance and then turned his face away in a rude gesture of dismissal.

Head held high, my mother marched out of the room, thinking, 'let him have his city without a Jew. We don't need any part of it!'

Later, she discussed the situation with my father and they decided that it would be better for me if we moved to another place. Their choice was Aleksandrow Kujawski, and we lived in that smaller city, from 1936-39.

I was eleven years old, at the time, and in the fifth grade of Catholic elementary school and was taught by the form master and teachers under him for various subjects. The form master's name was Blachowiak, who was a member of the Polish Nazi. Party, called the Endek party.

He was a very nice man, a good man, unfortunately he was also the product of hundreds of years of wrongful and unfounded teachings against the Jews, that had been drummed into his head; and one day, he began speaking about the Jews in a derogatory way, saying that they were a very cunning people, and gave an example, "Let us take the store that has just opened up by Jews. If you spend a certain amount, you get a gift. Now the Jews are smart, they take you in, the gifts they give you are no gifts, they are given to induce you to buy more than you need; in other words, they are fooling our poor."

What he was unaware of was that the new girl in the class, was the daughter of the storeowners, and upon hearing this, my heart began to race; it was my parents of whom he was speaking so badly, and I strongly had the need to put the record straight; and so I put up a hand to speak to him, and as soon as I was given permission to speak, I said, "I am sorry to tell you, but you have no idea about business because, giving gifts, in that way, is done in the Western world, and not just by the Jews but, people of all denominations, practise it."

Somewhat taken aback, as well, intrigued, a dialogue between us developed which was unheard of between a teacher and pupil, especially with one so young; because, in those days, children would never dare to contradict a teacher.

So I continued and said, "From the way you speak of Jewish business ethics, you are not very inclined towards us. But being a teacher, you must know the History of Poland better than I; so I would like to remind you that I have read the history of Poland, and it is said that the golden era of Poland started in the fourteenth century, when the King, Kasimiecz Wielki, alowed the Jews to enter Poland from Germany, and they brought them, not only money but business knowhow, and most important, they were tailors, shoe makers, tanners, furriers, and in all kinds of trade that changed Poland for the better."

While impressed, he was determined to defend his side of the argument, "But!" he replied, "They were not good soldiers that would fight for our beloved Poland."

Always a precocious child, I wouldn't give way. "Excuse me Sir!" I answered "What about Berek Yoseleivicz, a Jew. You must know that he won a very decisive battle for Poland."

Next day, Mr. Blachowiak came by my parents store, introduced himself as my teacher, and said, "I have come by because I wanted to know the parents of such a child. There is no way that she could have stood up to me, like that, with so much knowledge, for her age, unless she had special parents; and so I would like to become a friend of the family."

My parents exchanged glances, then my mother said, "Tell me, Mr. Blachowiak, do you play poker?"

Taken by surprise, he replied, "Yes!"

From then on, he was a regular visitor to our house for a game of Poker.

I enjoyed living in that small city; I also enjoyed life at school. Coming from an internationally famous capital such as Berlin, I was something of a celebrity to the small town girls, and they looked up to me; not that I wished it, but that was how it was, until that is, an incident occurred that, not only took me by surprise but, frightened me.

One of the girls, Jadviga, from the upper classes of society, approached me, one day, and said, "You know, Margota – they always put an 'a' at the end of my name, which in Poland, denotes a girl – "I would like to be friends with you, but when I think what your people did to our Lord Jesus, I cannot be your friend."

With a gasp, I hit back. "Listen, Jadviga, I am flattered that you would want to be friends with me, but I do not want to be friends with you because you are too stupid for me. What does it matter to you what happened two thousand years ago in a country where the people could read and write whilst your people, along with the rest of Europe, were still wandering about in the Dark Ages? First of all, we were under occupation by the Romans and thousands of Jews, as well as others, were put to death on the cross, and what happened to a Jew, like Jesus, back then, who fought the Romans on behalf of his people, is no business or concern of yours."

The girl's eye filled with horror and shaking from head to toe, she screamed, "Lord Jesus was not a Jew. How dare you mention his name."

It scared the life out of me. Every Jew in Poland knew that it was forbidden for them to mention his name and I felt sick with worry that my family might suffer because of what I had said.

That night, I went to bed without telling my parents what took place for fear of the catastrophe that may come about because of my thoughtlessness. I was devastated and couldn't sleep, turning this way and that my mind going over every single word that was spoken, again and again. Why didn't I keep my mouth shut? What was I thinking, I agonized over and over? It wasn't the people's fault that they believed the way they did. For hundreds of years, instead of teaching Christianity at its highest level of love and tolerance towards others, the church taught it at its lowest level and all they ever heard was hate, hate and more hate for the Jews.

What were the priests afraid of? That the truth might be revealed if, indeed, they followed the true teachings of the one they referred to as 'sweet Jesus'

Neither were they allowed to question as I was taught to do by the Rabbis. Their minds were kept closed and a closed mind can never bear the fruit of wisdom. ... My mind went back to when I went to bible classes in Berlin and the wonderful stories that came out of the Old Testament. My heart ached while reminiscing over the story of Jonah and the Whale. How we all laughed when we heard how he was thrown out of the fishes mouth onto dry land, crying, 'I am Jonah! I am Jonah!' and how no one knew who Jonah was. "It is a fable," said the rabbi without the least annoyance, "and one day you will understand the meaning of it."

All at once, I was struck by what he had said and understood, for the first time, that we were but tiny specks in the universe and should not take ourselves too seriously; We were as drops of water on the earth's surface, only to be dried up and, forever, be blown away by the wind. So how come the teachings of the church took a different view when enlightenment would have been to everyone's benefit? Why? Why? And what could, possibly, have been in the priest's mind to treat me like that?- His mind!-That was when I suddenly understood. I had always enjoyed history, and the bible was history, both the Old and the New Testament, and so, when I went to school in Poland, I would go to bible classes. The priest, mistakenly, took it as a sign that I was ripe for conversion, and it pleased his vanity. How was he going to feel now? I wondered, and the thought frightened me.

Priests always surrounded themselves with boys to serve them, and when I went to school, next morning, one of the boys was at the gate waiting for me.

"The priest wants to see you right away," he said with a rueful twist of his lips, and escorted me to his office.

Tentatively, I knocked on the door and opened it. But before I had a chance to put one foot in front of the other, the priest cried, putting a hand out to stop me, "Stay where you are. Don't you dare come anywhere near my desk.... Who told you that Jesus was a Jew ...? Your father?" and he spat the words out with such venom that it made me quake with fear.

Now I was a deep thinker, but not a quick one, nevertheless, I saw through him and knew what was in his mind, to put my father in prison for mentioning the name Jesus, which had dangerous consequences for a Jew, and, somehow, despite the terror in my heart, the right words came tumbling from my lips. "I came here one year ago from Germany, and in Germany, this is not a secret," I said, still quaking.

The priest glared at me. "What do you mean, you come from Germany? You speak a perfect Polish?"

"That's right, I have been here one year and I am quick to learn." I said.

The priest's eyes flashed with anger. "Get out of my sight," he screamed, "I don't want to look at you again."

Quietly, and with a sigh of relief, I closed the door behind me and made for my class

War, from the beginning of time, conjures up a picture of a battle field where a fight, between men equipped with the tools of war, was either won or lost. Boulders shot from giant slings, balls of fire that made their way into the compounds of soldiers; and arrows finding their mark in an arm, a leg, a heart.

Later came the advanced cannons, the muskets, killing and maiming, bringing death on the battlefields of men, standing up against men, whilst their families remained at a safe distance, in the city or town where they lived, their only fear being for their men folk doing battle for King and Country.

But life continuously evolves, as do the tools of war. The airplane made its mark during the First World War, and became the most violent tool of destruction during W W.11. It brought the battle to the streets of the cities – from the men at arms, to the babes in arms, blood running in the roads where once it ran in the fields where warriors gave their life for a cause.

We were still living in the city of Aleksandrow when the German occupation of Poland began commencing with heavy bombing flattening entire streets, stores, houses sending everyone into the streets in panic as we tried to escape the carnage by fleeing the city for safety, and making for Warsaw, bolting at full speed along the highway in thousands even as the German planes swooped down on us, the pilots, visible from the ground, firing their machineguns into the crowd, killing indiscriminately, anyone they had in their sights.

Unable to sleep, my father would walk the floor night after night, back and forth, back and forth, his mind a whirl of thoughts until he came to the decision to give the store away to my mother's brother. And going to Warsaw, to the Jewish legation, he bought the necessary papers that would enable us to leave Poland by ship and sail for Montevideo in Uruguay on September 29th. Too late, the Germans entered our city on the 28th and empounded the ship.

It was the foreplay to the entire German occupation of Poland that came swift and hard, leaving little time for anyone to escape their murderous plans.

My family and I were no exception and we ran along with the crowd until we realized there was no right or wrong way to turn; we were in the centre of a giant catastrophe with nowhere to run or hide from the massacre against us. And so, with heavy hearts, we did the only thing that was left to do, to return home and take whatever was in store for us.

Everything and everyone was in a turmoil and no-one more so than the Polish soldiers that, realizing, if caught in uniform, it would probably mean the firing squad, sought out stores that sold men's civilian clothing, leaving their guns and ammunition behind together with their uniforms, and joined the people along the route as one of them.

We found, when we returned, that our clothing store had been broken into, clothes were taken and in their place was a mountain of uniforms and a large cash of guns and ammunition. Along the route, the Germans had already posted notices that there would be an inspection of all premises and that, should anything be found other than that which the store had a right to sell, would be punishable, in all probability, by death. ...There was no time to lose before an inspection took place...!

My parents employed our caretaker, along with anyone else available, to swiftly gather up and get rid of the damning uniforms and weapons, leaving the store looking as it should, with nothing but the remaining civilian clothing. I ran down the street to see how close the German were and to determine how long we had to get the store back to normal before their arrival.

As I was rushing through the street, a German convoy of motorcyclists were already on its way. Now, no-one was allowed to be out on the street, and there was I, all alone, when one of the motorbikes, a young soldier at the front and a more mature officer with a huge pot belly, sitting in the side car of the vehicle that got out and called to me. This was not an S.S. convoy, but it was the wehrmacht, fortunately for me, and he said, 'You know you are not allowed to be out on the street...! Who are you...?'

I was fourteen years old, and foolishly looking him straight in the eyes, I replied with a proud lift of the head, 'I am a genuine Jewess...!'

The man looked as if the sky had just fallen on his head and his jaw dropped open and his eyes nearly popped out of their sockets in disbelief. '...You...you...' he blustered, 'you are lucky you said that to me...Don't ever say such a thing again... Now run away, quick...quick before I change my mind.' And I ran...!

Why good fortune was on my side, I had no idea; perhaps it was because I spoke to him in a cultured German and, being far away from home, he felt an affinity, but whatever it was, I was lucky.

When I returned home, I told my parents how far they were behind and it gave them enough time to do what was necessary. Soon after, the Germans gave the order that all stores were to be reopened immediately.

I never did tell my parents what happened. I realized that I had made a big mistake and that I had behaved stupidly. For a brief moment, I thought myself back in Germany with my friends, and coming from a liberal background to speak openly was normal for Jews before Hitler came to power.

Soon after, the Germans began their persecution of the Jews, and rounded up 360, who were told to leave their homes, taking with them only as much as they could carry, and they were herded onto one of those, now infamous, trains, to Majdanek which was one of the first concentration camps in Poland.

As yet, most were still unaware of the full extent to which the Germans would go in their plans to exterminate the Jews; still, it was terrifying for those remaining who sat in fear of what would happen to them. It was more so for me after having overheard my parents talking about what they should do, and that, if it were not for me, they would take their own lives before Hitler had a chance to take it from them. It was a responsibility that would bear heavily upon me, for I loved my parents dearly and feared losing them under any circumstances.

It was then that my father decided that it would be prudent to make plans in preparation for leaving Aleksandrow when it became necessary or when we were forced to leave by the Germans. We had some valuables that my parents wanted to save. As yet the occupying army didn't touch children or women and so it was planned that I would be the one to take these valuables to Lodz where we had relatives.

With the two valises' that my parents had filled with these precious items, I set out, by train, for Lodz where the goods were to be stored with our relatives. To get to Lodz from Aleksandrow I had to change trains at Wloclawek. On the return journey, again, I had to change trains at Wloclawek and while waiting for the train back to Aleksandow, I placed, the now empty suit cases on the station platform and sat on one, placing the other beside me.

No one really understood the complete scope of the disasters that were going on in the early days of the occupation; so I sat unaware of the danger that I was in, when, suddenly, the station master, already a young German officer probably raised in the Hitler youth movement to be placed in charge of the station – the younger they were the more vigilant and cruel they were - came out of his office and began circling me, his narrowed eyes on the two cases in my possession.

I had the yellow star on the back of my coat. Some Jews, when travelling, would remove them; but this was punishable in the worst of ways should they be discovered to be of the Jewish faith. Therefore, you were damned if you did and damned if you didn't. Either way, it was a dangerous practice and leaving the star on your coat was no guarantee of keeping you out of trouble.

Who knows what thoughts were going through the young soldiers head as he continued to circle me; but one thing was certain, seeing a young Jewess in charge of these two cases, he must have wondered what I could be hiding in them and he decided to find out. So he called me into the station office and demanded that I remove the cloth that my mother had placed over the expensive valises to try and hide them. No sooner his greedy eyes saw the expensive pig skin, than he demanded roughly, 'Give them to me at once,' and in place of them he threw me an old metal case that in Poland a religious Jew would have carried when travelling for business.

Being a young German girl, used to speaking with my neighbours in high German, without thinking I responded angrily, 'I don't understand this at all; you call us stinking Jews so if we stink then the cases, that I have held in my hands, must also stink...'

His eyes flared at me in rage and he screamed 'If you don't disappear this minute, I'll shoot you...'

I knew that he meant it, and without another thought, I ran...

When I got home with the cheap metal case, my parents weren't angry with me because they realized something must have happened; but when I told them the story, it upset my mother and she turned to my father and said, 'See what has happened... see what the war has done to her...? she is now lying to us because if she had said such a thing to a German officer, she would have been shot then and there.'

Shaking his head, my father replied, 'No! She has not lied to us, she was just foolish. When I was a young boy I too used to do stupid things. There was a war going on between Poland and Russia and I was in the city there, and my father didn't have an appetite to eat and I knew that he wanted some vodka to drink; so I used to run through the lines and over the fences while they were shooting at me just to get my father what he wanted. I could have been killed, but I didn't care because I was young and stupid and the young have no fear of death. So I know she didn't lie, she was just foolish; and we were foolish to have sent her to Lodz with valises filled with valuables, in the first place.

She is yet to learn fear; unfortunately, it is a lesson she will learn all too soon.'

I was present when my father spoke to his friends, telling them that life was going to be too cruel to survive.

"How come you talk like this in front of your daughter?" they asked.

"I haven't the luxury of telling her anything else," he replied.

It was heartbreaking. I was fourteen and on the verge of womanhood. How could it be happening? I wondered. Why had the rest of Europe waited so long before they stopped Hitler? Now that they had finally woken up, it was going to be a long hard battle, and in the meantime, the suffering of the innocent would go on and on, whilst I together with my parents were caught up in the middle of it all.

How often I thought If only we had followed David and his family to Palestine. How right he was to have left. Certainly it was going to be difficult for them in a country where the Arabs were against the Jews returning to their biblical home; but surely, it was going to be more difficult for those of us who stayed behind in Poland?

Where would it end? How would it end? I wondered.

At times, it was too painful to stand; at other times, I felt numb, as though I was sleep walking through a nightmare. It was on one of those numb occasions that I met a boy, on the street, that I knew from school. Apparently he had run so far, during the bombing, that he had left his parents behind and reached Bialystok to the east where the Russians had taken over Poland, whilst the Germans were in control of the west. But the line was yet to be established between them, leaving the border open. Now he had returned to look for his parents to take them back with him.

"Have you seen them," he asked me, his voice urgent with apprehension. "They must return with me.

The Russians don't kill Jews. I must find them at once before the border is closed."

Upon hearing this, I knew that I had to talk to my parents immediately; and in a rush, I cried, "I'm sorry, but I don't know where your parents are, I haven't seen them," and then rushed to get home as fast as I could.

While running, the sight of a wild eyed woman, with hair dishevelled, clothes in disarray, clutching a beautiful blue eyed boy to her chest like a baby, made me stop dead in my tracks and watch in terror as two members of the Gestapo, their dogs on a leash, apprehended the woman and snatched the child away from her, throwing it back and forth, to one another, as if it were a ball, all the while the boy crying, the mother screaming, "My baby, my baby," running from one to the other in an effort to retrieve her child while they continued to laugh.

I knew of this woman and how crazy she was; the whole town knew of her and that her husband was already on the Russian side having left earlier in fear of his life. As yet, the Germans didn't touch women and children.

I would have run away if I wasn't riveted to the spot watching in horror, when, suddenly, in a fit of desperation, the mother lunged at one of the brutes, and as tall as he was, managed to dig her long nails into his face and scratch it, enraging him to the point that he set his dogs on her and the child, that she had snatched away from them, tearing them to pieces, their horrifying screams, prompting me, out of sheer terror, to move my trembling legs, and run, the sound of the Gestapo's laughter following me down the street as I went.

Such incidences were happening, almost, on a daily basis. The whole town knew about them, some, like I, had witnessed the horrifying behaviour of the Gestapo, in broad daylight, that was sanctioned by Hitler on a people whose only crime was to be born a member of the Jewish faith.

Still distraught by the incident, as I entered our home I cried out, "Mama, Papa, we don't have to die! We don't have to die! There is a way out," and with excitement I explained to them what the boy had told me.

"My dear child," said my father, "I know about this, but I cannot live in Russia; it is a terrible country with that communism; they will kill me there, just as they will kill me here."

I was fraught with frustration. I wanted to run away and I wanted my parents to go with me; but my father was resisting. "Well I'm young and I don't want to die, I want to live," I cried. "If you don't go with me, I will go alone, and you know what happens to young girls on their own? They are raped and God knows what else. But I cannot live here in fear for my life, when I can be in a place where they don't persecute you for being a Jewess, even while it is bad for their own people."

My mother and father exchanged worried glances.... "You know," said my mother, "she is right, we have to do something about it."

It was soon after that something frightening happened that made them realize they had to make the decision to leave and quickly.

My mother used to buy meat from a Polish German, Herr Keller. There were many Germans who were born in Poland, in towns just across the border from Germany, and they spoke both languages. When the war came, those of German extraction were given special privileges and Herr Keller's daughter went to work at the office of the Oberleutnant – a high ranking German officer, and a list came into her hands, with the names of the ten most influential Jews, and one hundred Poles of the priesthood, including teachers, lawyers and landowners, the elite of Poland, that were to be shot.

It was nine in the evening, and my parents were still pondering the details of an escape, when there was a knock at the door. To their surprise, it was Herr Keller. No sooner had they invited him in to their home when he said, "I must tell you something. You know that my daughter works in the Oberleutnant's office and she has given me some information. There is a list of people that the Germans are going to shoot. I cannot tell you everything, because then they would realize that it must have come from someone in their office, but I am telling you, Herr Davidowitch, that you are on that list. You have to leave."

My father was not surprised; the German's had already sent the poorest of Jews of the town to Maijdanik, entering their homes, afterwards, to search for any usable objects, just like scavengers! It was only a matter of time before they got to him; now that time had come, but instead of sending him away, he was to be shot, leaving my mother and I in a desperate situation. Now, it seemed, there was some hope!

When my father saw how well inclined Herr Keller was towards us, he didn't question the reasoning behind it. When your life is at stake, who, but a fool, would question such a gift? But he did think, for a moment before saying, "I appreciate what you are doing, you are saving my life. How about going with me to Warsaw? I have some money that I dare not take with me, should the Gestapo board the train and begin asking questions. But, please, if you take it for me, we could meet at the station, in Warsaw, and I will give you ten percent of whatever there is."

Herr Keller didn't have to think twice and nodded, "Alright!"

The next day, leaving everything behind once again, while my mother stayed behind to organize things before meeting up with us in Warsaw, we took the train to the city where we met up with Herr Keller at the station. He was wearing the white arm band that the civilian Germans wore for identification, and he took my father aside and gave him the money, whilst I stood well back from where the transaction was taking place.

When it was completed, my father gave Herr Keller his ten percent, and then said to him.

"You have saved my life, now I am going to tell you something that will save yours. – As a Polish German, you have privileges. You run a profitable business, but you have not been treating the Polish butchers very well and they will not forget this. When the war is over, they will kill you."

Smiling, he replied, "I understand that you, being Jewish, have to think that way. But it will never happen. I am German, and this is the beginning of the thousand years Reich, as Hitler said it would be."

My father said no more.

As with all maniacs, Hitler's mesmerizing art of public speaking had made a deep impression on the minds of the German people.

I didn't return to Aleksandrow, after the war; but I did ask a friend, who was returning to the city, to find out what happened to Herr Keller – As my father predicted, he was killed by the Polish butchers who took their revenge for the infamous way in which he treated them during the war.

Fear, that most tormenting of all emotions, robs us of every other feeling by the sheer power that it holds over us and we become as animals on the street, doing whatever it takes to survive; sometimes envying those stray dogs that received more compassion from the Polish people, as they roamed the city, than the Jewish people who were in the same situation.

Once the transaction was taken care of, we went in search of a room in a poor, Jewish, district of Warsaw which, later, would be known as the 'Warsaw Ghetto'; a place where Jews lived and died in a brave attempt to continue on through the madness that engulfed Eastern Europe.

It was, already, an over-crowded area, owing to the notices that the Gestapo posted on huge bill boards, staring down at you, all over the city, giving the Jews two weeks to move into the designated area and to remain there.

"See what I mean!" exclaimed my father, "that's how it starts, and soon, there will be more restrictions, and God knows what else they have in store for us once they have us penned in like a flock of sheep…" Anyhow, he thought with a sigh, it was but for a short space of time whilst we decided on the best route to take across the border into the Russian sector.

By then, most of the border was closed and we had to find those, mostly peasants, who were familiar with the terrain and, for a price, would smuggle us across. As well, there was the need for one who could take our money over for us – To be caught with cash on your person meant certain death, or, at the best, you were relieved of it and sent back to Warsaw.

My father had noticed such people, with nothing to return to, living and dying on the streets after having given up their homes and taken as much as they could carry with them in the belief that they would never be returning to Warsaw. To see them begging, hungry and homeless with the cruel winds of winter biting into their tired bones was distressing, and my father understood that he could not let it happen to us.

So, after considering every aspect of our flight from certain death, it was decided, between my father and mother, who was now with us, that she would remain behind with the greater portion of our wealth, so that should my father and I get caught and be returned to Warsaw we would still have a place to live in and money to live on. As yet, it was only the men who faced death or mutilation at the hands of the Germans, and if we managed to get through without incident, we would send for my mother who would take the same route over the border into safety and then we would continue on to Bialystok, the chosen destination.

It was November and one of the coldest winters in memory, with the snow deep enough to cover an entire body that had been shot by one of the border guards either on the German side of a large area, which went for miles and known as 'no man's land', or the Russians who were just as quick to shoot anyone wanting to cross to their side of the border.

Anxious to know more about the escape route, my father asked the smuggler chosen to tell us how it was going to be done. "Look," said the man, "all you need to know is that I know what I am doing, and you must follow my instructions."

We didn't realize it then, but had the man told us exactly how it was going to happen, my father would have thought twice about leaving; so it worked to our advantage not to know beforehand.

However, he did warn us that, at the station, in Warsaw, before we boarded the train where we were to meet him, there would be many Poles standing on the platform, waiting for the Jews who were anxious to escape, and they would approach us with blackmail, demanding 20 or thirty zlotys, or they would inform the Germans that there were Jews at the station ready to leave. And so we had to prepare enough cash to save ourselves from being given away by heartless people.

When the time arrived, it was with the greatest sorrow that my father and I bade my mother goodbye. If a knife had been plunged into our hearts it could not have been more painful and we had to steel ourselves to leave, in the belief that, one way or another, we would soon be together again. And thus, under cover of darkness, our hearts heavy, we made our way to the station.

We found many Jewish people there seeking to escape as we were, faces solemn, eyes mirroring their despair. For them, there was no such thing as hope; hope was for the fortunate, not for those who were suffering through one of history's darkest periods.

It was a lucrative business for the local farmers, now smugglers, who would herd us onto the trains, placing us into compartments allocated to each smuggler. Tickets were for the border town of Malkinia, and everyone settled down thinking it wouldn't be long before we reached the safety of that particular city. It was not to be! Just minutes before we were due to reach our destination, the order was given, by the smuggler, to jump out of the windows of the moving train, once it had slowed down enough but not stopped. 'This is important,' he told us, 'because you don't want to come face to face with the German police who are aware of what is going on, and are waiting at the station with guns, ready to shoot you.

There was a gasp of disbelief – the windows of a Pullman carriage were barely large enough for a child to pass through, and with the rucksacks strapped to our backs, it seemed impossible. Impossible or not, the scramble to safety soon began. Only seconds could have passed, but it seemed like an age before my father and I were following a man and his wife that managed to crawl through the windows that had been shattered in their hurry, and compressing ourselves as tightly as possible, we managed to squeeze through, but not without cuts on our hands and ripping the cloth of our coats on the broken glass.

There was no moon, that night, and it was only when we dropped from the moving train onto hard steel that we realized there were more lines filled with stationary wagons before we could reach 'no man's land'. Suddenly, shots rang out followed by the shrill screams of those that had been hit - The German's were there waiting for us and they showed no mercy.

People were crawling, on their bellies, beneath the dormant wagons, trying to dodge the bullets that came fast and furiously as machine guns were used to fire under the trains. Some made it, many didn't; either way, it was a horrifying experience, especially for the aged such as my father who was fifty six and feeling every bit of it. It was obvious that, all along, the German's knew about the repeated escapes that were going on, and my mouth dried up with fear for both myself and my father.

All at once, the shooting stopped. Those of us that survived the ordeal had reached the free zone and there would be no more bullets from German guns. Nevertheless, it was a harsh winter with snow well above the ankles, making the trek to the other side as hazardous as dodging the bullets.

Suddenly, people were joining us from all sides, dark shadows against the white snow, swelling the numbers to -50- 60-100-and still they came; men, women, children clinging to their mother's skirts, babes in arms, trudging, trudging through the snow with the fixed eye and tight jaw of the determined. They had made it so far, they were going to make it all the way.

The smugglers insisted that we keep up with them if we didn't want to freeze to death in 'no man's land'. My father and I had but one thought, to survive against all odds, and we drove one foot after the other, deeper and deeper into the snow, whilst the sweat was pouring off us from the weight of the rucksacks and the layers of clothes on our backs.

My only worry was losing sight of my father who was trying, desperately, to keep up with me and if it were not for the white of the snow, it would have been difficult to make out his form in the, black, freezing air that made it difficult to take a breath without pain from its icy attack on our chests.

All at once, the distant thunder of hooves filled our ears, growing louder and louder as a number of horsemen came bearing down on us; and before we realized it, we were surrounded by the mounted Russian border police who were cursing and swearing as they circled the exhausted gathering, containing us in a ring as they might contain a herd of wild animals. Then they closed in even further until the tight crowd could smell the steaming breath of the restless horses; and there we stood, motionless, until suddenly, breaking ranks, the police gave the order, 'follow' and off they sped, leading us, the tired and frozen men, women and children for miles, their whips lashing through the air with a fearful crack, driving their mounts faster and faster. It gave us no time to consider, no time to realize how impossible the task of following the mounted soldiers would be; for us it was do or die in the frozen ground and our legs began moving in out, in out, like puppets on a string, left right, left right, as fast as the driven snow would allow our legs to, our breath escaping in short sharp bursts as we scrambled to follow as if the whips were lashing our backs, instead of the horses, in order to keep us going.

Ready to drop, our knees buckling with exhaustion, we came to a huge barn and were lead inside. The interior was as dark as it was outside, with air so thick and foul that it could be cut through with a knife, and there we remained for two days and two nights without food or water, sick with hunger and too tired and dry mouthed to complain.

On the third day, the doors suddenly opened, the day light blinding us until we became used to the brightness, and guards, known as the NKVD entered and made us drag our stiff and weary bones from where we were sitting on the dirt floor, to form lines in readiness for questions that were designed more to trick us than to help us.

Back in Warsaw, my father had heard of such questions and knew that some people succeeded in their quest to go to the Russian zone, whilst others didn't, and the thought was daunting. He knew we had to succeed, but how? That was a different question.

It so happened, that when we were put inside the barn, my father and I found ourselves sitting next to a man and his daughter, the man's wife having been shot by the Germans whilst crossing the railway lines, and we discovered, they were not only the same ages as we were, but were of a similar background, and we spent the time discussing as much as our dry, croaking, voices would permit.

"You know," said my father, "I heard in Warsaw, that if you told the Russians you wanted to go to Bialystok, they send you to Warsaw, and if you say Warsaw, they send you to Bialystok. You never know with these Russians, they are always tricking you."

"I was thinking about this," replied the man. "but I'm sure I can manage the situation to our advantage. I am a Russian Jew, I ran away after the revolution. I still speak a good Russian, and I understand their mentality; so I am going to tell you what you must do. You must take your daughter and pretend you are both something of an imbecile and they will find this funny and laugh and it will put them off guard; I will be behind you and I will go up to them and say, in Russian, ' You can see who you are dealing with, but I have spoken with this man and he told me what he wanted. He wants to go to the German occupation and bring his wife back to Russia with him'. I will not name the city, this time, I will play with them."

"So what does it mean?" asked my father. "I don't understand."

"It means they will believe you come from Russia, and that they wouldn't allow you to bring your wife from Germany into Russia, and so they will place you in the line of the city where they are going to send you; and I will know, from that, if it is the same city where I want to go and, if so, I will understand what I must do."

Giving it some thought, my father said, "…Yes, I can see that is the only way it will work."

Having done some acting, my father, instinctively, knew how to portray himself. And so, hunching his shoulders, shuffling his feet along the ground, his mouth loose and drooping, he walked with me beside him, following his lead, up to the guard in charge, both of us dribbling and uttering strange incoherent sounds.

The ridiculous sight of us, supposed, idiots made him smirk, and he asked, in Russian, "Where to?"

We couldn't understand a word of what he was saying, anyhow, and made some strange, exaggerated, faces in response.

Thinking us still funnier, he roared with laughter, and that is when, as planned, the man came forward. "I can see what your difficulty is with these people," he said, "but he told me, in his simple way, where they are coming from and where they want to go, so I will tell you, exactly, word for word, what was said. The father wants to go to the German side to fetch his wife and take her back to Russia with him. So that is why he must go to the German Zone, for his wife."

The guard, eyeing such a strange looking pair, continued to find it amusing and decided to have some fun with us. "Look," he said to my father, thoroughly enjoying the game he was playing, "You don't need to go there, you don`t need to bring a woman back with you, there are plenty of women for you in Russia," all the time thinking ... 'who would want to marry such an idiot' and he then sent us to the line that would take us to the Russian side, the opposite of what he believed we wanted.

Afterwards, shaking his head in disbelief, my father turned to the man who saved us and said, "... I've never lied in my life; yet, when it came to be or not to be, I lied...!"

"Don't you worry about it," he replied, "I fooled them without having to mention any city in Russia or Germany; and because of the good mood you put them in with your act, you were placed in the right line without them realizing it; and from that, I knew exactly what I had to say to be placed in the same line.

There was another line formed of many young women with babes in arms who had asked to be sent to the Russian side where their husbands were waiting for them; but telling the truth was their undoing and they were now in that line that would take them back to Warsaw.

There are times, in life, when there comes a moment when, instinctively, you know that you are in danger such as in the wrong place at the wrong time and that was one of them; and when the guards told them to move they, defiantly, stayed put, not daring to budge an inch; but the guards didn't care that they were women and little children, and when they began shooting at them, they had no choice but to return to 'no man's land' despite the fact that they and their children faced certain death in the bitter cold.

Later, it was learned that, twenty thousand Jews, unable to go back to the German side, and unable to return to the Russian side, had frozen solid, in that bitter waste land, and the women and their babies, clutched to their bosom for warmth, were part of that number to die such a terrible death, leaving behind a field of monuments to the perverse cruelty of the Russian border guards. Nevertheless, there were some that survived those savage winds and freezing temperatures and, instead of dying, lost limbs, mostly feet and hands, to frost bite, that later had to be amputated to save them from gangrene and eventual death.

That is how it must have been for many of those in the concentration camps; people, suddenly, confronted by what it meant to be in a particular line. We can never begin to imagine what horrors went through their minds, or if, somehow, their brains managed to shut down altogether, leaving them numb in the face of what, they knew, was to be.

It leaves us, the fortunate, wondering what those concentration camp guards, that held life and death in their hands, were about. But there are no words, heinous enough, to describe they who had the nerve, the effrontery, the offensiveness to still consider themselves members of the human race.

When we reached Bialystok, my father and I looked up the address we were given by the Jewish currency smuggler who was to take our money across the border for us. Going up the steps to the front door, we knocked. A maid answered. It was just the beginning of the Russian occupation and, as yet, house maids had not been forbidden to serve in the homes of wealthy Jews, and she lead us in to the living room where we waited to see the owners of the beautifully appointed apartment.

From the moment the couple entered the room, the woman tall and stately wearing a string of real pearls around her slender throat and her husband, equally as tall and distinguished with black hair and greying sideburns, it was obvious to my father that they were very cultured people that, in all probability, as so many cultured Europeans did, could converse in many languages; and so my father addressed them in German, and explained why we were there, showing them the piece of paper with their address written on it by the man who was living in their home.

The moment they took the paper in their hands they went white and were unable to utter a word, they were so embarrassed that, immediately, my father realized that something was very wrong. ... Heart in mouth, he asked, "Please don't spare me, one way or another, you have to tell me what it is; I must know!"

Swallowing, the woman whispered "... I am afraid that he has been shot and so there is no money for you...." But then, recognizing the calibre of the man they were speaking to, the woman suddenly said, "If you wait a moment, I will speak to my husband." And she took him by the arm and lead him into the next room, leaving us alone and anxious.

Beside himself with worry, so strained was he that my father feared he might have a heart attack.... What were they going to do now? They had nothing! Nothing! How would they live? What was more, there was no way they could bring my mother across the border, they were completely closed.... It was heart wrenching, a nightmare that we hadn't counted on, and we were desperate.

Shortly, the couple returned. ... "Neither of us feel that we can allow you to just go out on the street with nothing in your pocket; it's not for people like you," said the woman "We have a room that the gentleman you were supposed to meet, used to stay in whilst over here. It is now vacant and we would like you to have it for as long as you like, there will be no charge."

My father knew, that a room in such a good home could fetch a fortune, any room, at that time, was difficult to come by, so he was overwhelmed by their kindness and, with a sigh of relief, accepted their offer graciously.

Immediately after settling in, we took whatever jewellery we had, such as rings, and went to the market place in search of someone who would buy them, so that we would have a little money for food. Before returning to our room, my father decided we would spend whatever we had left on a treat – we needed something, anything to make us feel human again, and so we went to a coffee house where we indulged ourselves with coffee and cake, wondering when we would next enjoy such a luxury.

As we sat there, pondering our fate, my father heard his name being called with some excitement. "Davidowitch! Davidowitch!! What are you doing here?"

He turned and saw a friend of his from Berlin, Wagner, a man he had helped to become very wealthy in the days when he had pull; and he told him our story. "Now I am spending my last penny on a cup of coffee and a piece of cake." He announced raising his brow as if to say, so there it is!

He placed a comforting hand on my father's shoulder. "After what you did for Wagner, Davidowitch will never have to spend his last penny on a piece of cake," he cried "I am the biggest contrabandist in Bialystok. I occupy a whole rooming house for my activities and you can live off me forever,"

"It is very nice of you," said my father "but I couldn't do that. What you can do is give me the merchandise that you give others and I will sell it for you to make a living."

Wagner smiled, "You are not the type! You know what we used to call you in the business, 'The Gentleman' you were so straight."

"That was then, but now is now and that is how it has to be!" replied my father.

So Wagner had no choice but to do as he asked, and, however reluctantly, he gave him the materials to sell.

My father, who had been a representative of a huge textile mill, dealt with the manufacturers who would make the materials up into clothes ready to sell to the big stores and smaller store chains that sold directly to the public. He was good, so good that he was always being offered top positions at other mills; What made him so good? He had an inner sense about people, whom he could trust and whom he couldn't and it was an asset that was coveted by others in the industry; but he was loyal and always refused, no matter what the incentive. At the other end of the scale, doing business with the average house wife, out searching for a bargain in the local market place, was as foreign to him as chalk is to cheese; but he, desperately, needed to make a living if we were to survive. Therefore, he had no alternative but to adapt himself to the situation and do what was needed to be done in the only manner that was possible for him – to put on an act. After all, hadn't he acted on stage, if only as an amateur, it was still acting, and he had been good at it?

Tacking it to the next stage, my father decided to play the part as a character out of a Shakespeare play, and draping the colourful materials about his shoulders, as they might have done in Elizabethan times, he ventured forth, ready to attract the passerby and make a sale.

In those days, in communist Russia, people who had contraband to sell would place them under their coat and not on their back, but my father was innocent of the ways of such matters, and he not only caught the attention of the locals, but of those who were in the same business as Wagner. They were from Lodz, where they manufactured clothes, and remembered my father who used to buy goods from them, for his clothing store; and knowing him well, they feared for themselves and went to see Wagner. "What are you doing?" they cried, "You could have given him anything to keep him out of the market, he is too Westernized in his ways, too honest, he's no match for the shrewd Russians; he will get us all into trouble."

"What could I do," said Wagner, "he wouldn't have it any other way. I had to help him."

This went on for a few days and, sure enough, my father was caught by the police. When the others saw what happened, they ran around to Wagner immediately, to inform him that Simon was in custody.

When he heard this, he said, "I will have to leave at once. I know this man, he always had difficulty in lying, and under pressure, he will give me away and I cannot stay here another minute."

Fortunately, Wagner knew, that what he was doing couldn't last forever, and had prepared himself for such a time, and, in ten minutes, he was gone.

Meanwhile, at the police station, because of his lack of Russian, they had a Jewish ENKWD. (political policeman}, who spoke Yiddish, to speak to my father and find out as much as he could.

"I have a daughter with me," said my father, "I have to be with her."

"Then you must listen to me," said the ENKWD. "If you want to see your daughter again, you had better tell them who you are working for or you will both be dead."

After hearing that, my father, who always had strong moral convictions, lost no time in giving them what they wanted. After all, his daughter was of greater importance to him than a principle.

With what had happened, my father realized that we could no longer stay in Bialystok and so he looked to his niece, Leah and her husband Lazar, who lived in the village of Yanow on the borders with Russia, and that is where we made for.... He also realized that, at some stage, the Germans would invade that particular area of Russia. But that was in the future. In the meantime we would have some peace and time to consider what our next move had to be.

Now Lazar had been a watchmaker in Gdynia where he had a jewellery store and also sold and repaired watches. One day, when business was slow, he was standing on the sidewalk outside the store when he noticed a commotion going on between a Russian captain of a warship that was in the harbour, and some Polish people. He had apparently lost his way and was trying to find out the way back to the harbour, but he couldn't speak Polish, and they couldn't speak Russian.

When Lazar saw what was happening, and being able to speak fluent Russian, through his parents, who after having escaped the Russian revolution settled in the eastern part of Poland with their sons, each of whom located in different cities as watchmakers, he approached the captain and asked, in fluent Russian, what it was that he wanted to know.

Somewhat surprised, he said, "I have lost my way and would like to get back to my ship... But tell me, how is it that you speak such a good Russian?"

Lazar replied, "My parents were originally from Kalenin in Russia and they ran from the revolution, but we still speak Russian at home."

Upon hearing this, the captain's eyes opened wide in disbelief. "Kalenin...?" he cried. "What's your name? What's your family name...?"

"Komisarchik" said Lazar, "Why?"

"My God...!" He said, looking as if he was in some kind of fantasy. "I am Komisarchik...I am from Kalenin..."

Lazar searched his face and suddenly recognised him from a photograph that his father kept of his family, back in Russia, because his younger brothers didn't run from the revolution, as he did and remained behind; and while speaking with each other, it came to them that they were uncle and nephew, and throwing their arms around each other in excitement they embraced, giving each other huge kisses on each cheek, over and over again.

Of course the captain invited Lazar and his wife to join the ship every evening for a party, while they were in harbour, which was for a week.

A few days after the ship had left, Lazar received notice from the Polish authority, that he was suspected of communism and was to be banished from that city and everywhere else in Poland except one place that was in East Poland on the borders with Russia, and so they were exiled to Yanow that was close to the city of Pinsk; and there and only there were they allowed to live.

They had to move immediately, leaving everything behind; and while in Yanow, Lazar opened, a much smaller store than the one he had in Gdynia, and sold and repaired wrist watches. And that is where my father and I fled, to the town of Yanow, to join my father's cousin Leah and her husband Lazar.

While living with them, the Russians decided that all Polish citizens living in Yanow, that was now a Russian occupied zone, had to register, and when my father and I were brought before them, we were asked if we wanted a Russian passport.

My father feared that by owning a Russian passport, we would become Russian citizens forever and that he didn't want. So, unaware of what the repercussions might be, he refused their offer.

Now Leah's husband, Lazar, who once again was repairing watches for a living, had amongst his clients members of the Russian authority. In fact, Russians so loved wristwatches, that it was not unusual to see them wearing as many as two, three or even more, different kinds of wristwatches, on their arms.

Whilst visiting the offices of the authority, a vital piece of information came Lazar's way. There was going to be a purge and all Polish citizens, that didn't have Russian passports, were going to be picked up, as politically undesirables, and sent to a gulag in the very north of Russia.

The moment he returned home, Lazar had a meeting with his wife and my father. "Listen," he said. "The Russian authority is preparing to pick you up and transport you to a gulag. Now Margot is fourteen and so they will leave her alone, but you, Simon, are in trouble and must go away from here. Now there is a farmer, that I know, and he will let you stay with him, but we must leave tonight."

And so, after dark, he got out his horse and buggy, and driving the horse as fast as was possible, they came to the farmhouse where he left my father and returned home.

The very next day two Russian members of the authority, one being of Jewish heritage that thought of himself as a good communist before being a good Jew, came to the house, and would have turned away, when my father was nowhere to be found, if it had not been for the Jew who put forward an idea to his partner. He suspected that Lazar, being friendly with members of the communist party, had learned, from them, that there was to be a purge, and so hid the father away somewhere.

"We will take the daughter, "he said, "and when the father hears this, he will want to be with her and rush back from wherever he is; and then we will have them both."

Naturally, when they took me, Lazar rushed to tell my father what happened, whereupon he rushed back and went straight to the railways station where the train that held me was waiting, and with a sigh of relief, got into the carriage with me.

Minutes before the train left, he turned to Lazar, who was standing on the platform looking most upset, and said, "You know, this may not be such a bad thing that is happening to us, it may very well save our lives. The Germans will soon invade this part of Poland and he will kill all the Jews here. You should take your family and leave for Russia as soon as possible."

Unfortunately, as soon as possible, was not soon enough, and when the Germans came, Lazar and his family, along with all the other Jews, were taken to the market place, and shot.

On the train, that took many days reaching its destination, were three groups of Polish Jews; the professionals, such as doctors, lawyers, scientists, etc., people of privilege that had never done a menial days work in their lives. Then there were the middle class that came from every walk of life and were used to dealing with difficult circumstances and had some knowledge of hard work. The third being those of an unlawful nature such as thieves and crooks of one kind or another.

It has always been natural for people to gravitate towards those of a similar background that separated one class from another. But my father was a unique person that could mix equally well with every kind of human being, and he became very friendly with a doctor, that had studied medicine in Berlin, who took an instant liking to him and me with whom he had a lot in common.

"You will be with us in our barrack," said the doctor to my father.

Now my father was no fool; under normal circumstances he would have been delighted to be put in the same barrack as the professional class; but he realized that those people were not equipped for such a life as they would have to lead under the guard of the Russians who would put them to hard labour. He knew where we would be better off, amongst those that would know how to put their nose to the grindstone and would have had some experience in the field of manual work. In fact, if he had a choice, my father would have put his lot in with the criminal class, for they knew well, how to look after themselves.

When the train finally arrived at its destination, and the gulag which was situated in the middle of a clearing in the forest where three wooden barracks were placed, as well a house for the commandant that would be overseeing us, his job being to make certain that no one escaped; not that there was any chance of escaping in that baron wasteland, my father, saying nothing to the doctor, slipped away to assess what the right thing to do would be, in such a situation. Meanwhile, the doctor told me to go with him, as he was certain that my father would follow.

While looking around for my father, I heard my name being whispered, and recognized the voice as my fathers; and going to him, I said, "Where did you go? Why aren't you with us?"

"Firstly, Margot, you follow me and remain close at all times. Secondly, these professional people have no idea how to survive and will only argue with each other and end up in complete disarray."

And so we stayed with those that came from all walks of life, and could cope with the hardships as they found them and my father told them that he had never done any hard work before, and that they would have to guide him. "Don't worry," they said, "We will help you all we can.

Of course, as my father predicted, the professionals ended up in trouble, arguing and accusing each other of not pulling their weight.

One day, the doctor came to my father and said, "You are a very wise man; you knew what would happen between us and so you left us for the group better able to do what is necessary. But I have spoken to the authorities and explained that there were some of us that are too old for manual labour and needed to be given lighter duties, and they agreed. How would you like to join this group amongst us?"

Of course, my father was delighted and immediately agreed to join them.

Now there was an American man that was politically unaware of the dangers in entering that part of Poland that would soon be occupied by the Russians. He had taken his family to Poland to visit his parents and was still there when the Russians arrived. No matter that they held American passports, they were Polish by birth, and as such, The Russians considered them politically undesirable just like everyone else of Polish descent.

However, letters and parcels from America were allowed to enter the country and be received by those held in a Russian gulag. When the family, back in America, heard what happened to them, they sent parcels of food containing tins of meat, fish, fruit and whatever else that wasn't perishable. The gentleman, Mr. Weinburg, being of a good heart, would offer my father some of the food for him and and me to partake.

As much as he would have liked to accept such gifts, my father declared, "I cannot take any of this necessary food that you and your family badly need to survive; and besides, you have no idea when these parcels will stop coming."

Mr. Weinburg, waving such arguments aside said, "Please...I beg you, take it. ... I will tell you something; you and I will not survive this situation. So what difference does it make if you should enjoy a little extra comfort from what I bring for you and your daughter?"

So put like that, my father, gratefully, took the treasured tins of meat to give to me in an effort to stave off hunger, if only for a while.

In the end, as he said it would be, neither the man nor my father managed to survive.

The gulag we were sent to was in the province of Archangelsk in the North Pole, on the border with Finland where winter would persist for nine months of the year with temperatures dropping as low as minus 30%. Summer was barely more comfortable with the snow melting and forming lakes of water, leaving little dry land to grow anything of value that would provide a balanced diet and, scurvy, especially amongst those interned in the gulag, was a big worry.

The summer, was known as the 'white nights' - because of the sun that shone for 24 hours a day for three months, as opposed to the winter, when it was dark, 24 hours a day, for three months, leaving the rest of the year in a state of in-between, with long nights and short days, in a land of cruel contrasts.

The living conditions in the gulag was primitive, to say the least, and was arranged in three barracks, sleeping 31 people in each, and a large hall in the centre of the compound for all other activities that were, not only for them, but for the local folk as well.

Families were kept together, sleeping on wooden bunks without a mattress or pillow on which to lay their heads and they would use a coat, or anything else they could find to make it more bearable. The blankets we were given had been used by previous occupants and were full of lice. As well, blankets were hung over lines, separating families, for a modicum of privacy. Privacy! There was no such thing in a gulag and you could consider yourselves fortunate, if you got on with your fellow inmates; but then it was do or suffer and they had all suffered enough. We did, however, make friend with another couple.

If, under the circumstances, it wasn't exactly the sort of companionship of like minds, it did make our lives somewhat more bearable.

Meals were taken in the central hall, at long wooden trestle tables with seats of long wooden benches either side. It was, in fact, a wooden barrack that was not only used for meals, such as they were, for the inmates of the gulag, but also for entertainment, where the locals would come, over the week-end, to dance and, generally have a good time. Despite what I was going through, I also had a good time, simply, watching them dancing still dressed in their long, cumbersome coats, fur hats and boots that were worn in winter. It all seemed so incongruous to me and made me laugh.

While breakfast consisted of a stale chunk of bread and a cup of hot water. The mid-day meal, usually out in the forest where we worked, was two slices of bread with something unrecognisable between them. Supper was just enough to stave off complete hunger so that we could keep on going and doing what was expected of us.

In the beginning, I would dream of eating apples, oranges, bananas, but soon I was too hungry to even dream and would eat whatever was before me, no matter how tasteless or foul, anything just to fill the empty, nagging space in my stomach. There were so many empty spaces inside me, back then, with nothing to fill them, not my brain, not my heart or soul, as though I was already dead without thought or feeling – feeling was the treat of a full stomach. An empty belly signals the demise of all the senses except for the pangs of hunger and even that soon disappears along with the gnawing pain that sees no point in reminding you of your hunger when there's nothing to quieten it sufficiently and gives up; and, it seemed to me, that I would never again enjoy a full stomach. I was not alone; it was the same for all the internees, so how could I complain or feel sorry for myself; feeling sorry for yourself was another of those luxuries reserved for the more fortunate.

The men and women worked hard and long; every day, summer and winter when the snow was knee high and they had no clothing for protection against the freezing conditions, we had to walk six miles to and from the forests, cutting down trees whilst the women collected the branches, throwing them onto a bonfire. Under normal circumstances, it was a job for the hardiest of men, and with little sustenance to keep them going, it took its toll on many of them.

Not far from where we toiled in the forest, there was a gulag for hardened criminals, who also worked in the forest, under different commandants. Sometimes, during a break from work, when we would eat handfuls of snow for water, we would meet up with them and talk to each other. The convicts were interested in us because we were not Russian and they wanted to know all about us and how come we were there. And we found the convicts interesting, with their strange and frightening looks of the vicious animals that they were; and we would ask them questions, one in particular that we found intriguing.

"What is the worst punishment for a criminal? Is it the death sentence, or what?" We asked.

They replied, 'The biggest punishment for us is not the death sentence, but hard labour and the discipline that goes with it, to get up early in the morning to do a day's work; it doesn't suit our character. We don't like hard work and we don't like discipline. And that is why," they said, "there are not so many hardened criminals in Stalin's Russia, because they are more afraid of the gulag than being put to death and Stalin knows this."

There was no reason to disbelieve them. They told the truth, they had nothing to lose. They preferred crime over work and knew that they would never be released from there.

The worst time was in the summer months when clouds of the tiniest flies would swarm around us, entering our eyes, nose, mouths and ears, whilst we shook our heads from side to side and waved our arms about in an effort to fight them off, but to no avail.

Sometimes, it got so bad that we felt we couldn't carry on; but we did, not just because we had no choice, but we had a burning desire to live to see the day when Hitler lost the war and was brought to justice, which we were certain of; and it kept us going under the worst circumstances.

The guards, who were sent to watch us and make sure there was no slacking, did their job well, as they did from morning to night; they were always there, watching and watching and keeping us in order, allowing us no freedom whatsoever; not that we could have done anything with freedom, we were in the middle of nowhere.

One day, the flies were so bad, that a man and his son, unable to bear it any longer, simply dropped their tools and wandered deeper into the forest. Later, they were found, their necks broken, their limp bodies dangling from a tree, flies buzzing around them. They had hanged themselves. There were some who would have, gladly, changed places with them, yet, in the final analysis, life is life no matter how difficult.[1]

Red spots from small, broken, blood vessels began to appear beneath the surface of my father's skin and his gums were swollen and bleeding. He had, what everyone feared most, the deadly scurvy.

While it hit me hard, I had my own problems. After complaining of feverish headaches and a rash over my body, as well as to the extremities, arms, legs, soles of my feet, I was found to be suffering from typhus, which I contracted from the lice that were everywhere, our clothes, our hair, and was sent to an infirmary with nineteen others, in the same condition. The attention was poor and medicines, virtually, nonexistent and seventeen of us died, I was one of the two lucky ones that survived.

While I had been delirious and hallucinating, during unconsciousness, shouting and cursing Stalin, in my fever, the nurse, that was looking after me and who hated Stalin every bit as much as I, felt a kindred spirit towards me, and having taken a liking to me, made sure that I had enough to eat by stealing the jelly and medicine that came from America for the Russian officers, and gave them to me, pushing the Jelly down my throat to make sure I got the very last ounce of it.

When I came out of my delirium, the nurse told me, 'You are my girl; I did what I could to save you.'

When I asked "How come?" she replied, "I hate Stalin as much as you do and so I grew attached to you and wanted to

---

[1] When I saw the vast amount of crime in American, and how, comparatively, comfortable the conditions of the prisons were for the criminals, I realized that punishment in Russia, was the single, lone, factor of communism that made any sense.

save you at all cost. Don't you remember me sitting by your side and pushing as much jelly into your mouth as you could eat?"

Suddenly, I remembered it as it happened.

After the typhus, I was deaf for three months before I regained my hearing, but not my balance that comes from the middle ear. To this day, I still suffers from the affliction and have to be careful of falling.

And that is how we lived for fourteen months, until the Americans came into the war, and a temporary Polish embassy was set up in London, when negotiations began to procure the freedom of the Polish citizens that had been interned by the Russians.

A delegation was formed to deal with the matter, and the commandant of the gulag gave us the identification papers needed for traveling.

Unable to speak Russian himself, my father asked me, as I did speak the language, to ask the commandant where he would suggest we could travel, in Russia, as free people.

With an ironic smile, the commandant replied, "In communist Russia? There are no good places – but I will write, on your papers, that you can travel to Alma Tar which is close to the Iranian border where the climate is good and everything grows all year round.

Unfortunately, my father and I were not destined to make it. We had to take a train to Kirov and then another to Alma Tar, but somewhere along the route, our papers were stolen, and it was impossible to board a train without them. It would also have been physically impossible, it was so crowded with people from all over, and besides, my father was too ill and I still too weak and swollen from the typhus. Neither could we get a piece of bread without the papers, and at night we were made to leave the shelter of the station so that it could be cleaned of the filth and lice everyone carried with them from wherever they came from, and we were thrown out into the street where, being September, it was already cold and raining.

We had no choice but to report to the police and tell them what had happened to us and the police sent us to a small village, close to Kirov, where the locals took their meals in a building that had a large dining hall that was also for recreation.

It was a small village of peasants, where each of them had their own little home and, whatever they earned, belonged to the village, like in a commune. There were not only Jews, that were sent there, but Lithuanians and Latvians amongst others, and the peasants, of the village, were not happy about it and would go around asking people where they came from and what nationality they were. When they came to me and my father, we told them, we are Jews, and immediately the people went into shock. Eventually, coming to themselves, they began to circle us, looking us over from top to toe, as if they were searching for something that would confirm who we were.

Suddenly, one of the villagers said, "Why do you say that you are Jews? You are not Jews, you don't have horns!"

In disbelief, I looked them in the eyes and asked, "What are you talking about? How could human beings have horns?"

They looked at one another in confusion – "But we were told by the church that Jews were devils, and devils have horns."

If they had finally come to understand that there must have been a misunderstanding, it did little to change their minds about the situation and they complained bitterly about it.

At the end of the day, an elder of the community, came to place the refugees, who arrived from all over Eastern Russia, into the homes of the villagers; placing me and my father with a widow, whose two son were in a position of importance in the communist party, and were away from home at the time.

The widow was most unhappy, and although she had never met a Jew before, she told the elders that she didn't like Jews and didn't want them in her home.

"Listen, Vasila" said the elder, "you are an ignorant woman. I was in the First World War, a Russian soldier in Poland where I met a lot of Jews. I am giving these people to you because I want you to be alright. Jews do not steal the way our people do; so you listen to me, old woman that you are, and be pleased with the choice I gave you. Later, you will be grateful to me."

While still unhappy with the situation, she heard, from others in the village, that the people placed with them were stealing – stealing! What could they steal but a potato or an onion, but a potato and an onion were like gold and silver to a hungry peasant who depended on them for survival.

My father was suffering terribly from scurvy, and then there was the 'chicken blindness' - night blindness -that both of us were suffering from, which the villagers helped to cure by making us eat cakes of frozen ox blood; there were no carrots, not even one could be found. But the peasants knew what they were doing and, miraculously, it worked.

It happened, that close to the village, there was a black market place where the peasants would sell whatever they could lay their hands on, to those willing to pay their price, in order to survive a harsh existence.

On one such day, when my father went to the market place to buy bread, he noticed a peculiar family, one that he had never seen before. They were a mother, father, one daughter and three sons, who, apart from the daughter who looked normal, they were the strangest looking people he had ever come across. They were huge, wild, black eyed with crooked mouths and grotesquely proportioned figures.

Who were these forbidding people, wondered my father. Could they possibly be Polish gypsies? But being of an unbiased nature, he soon dismissed the thought as unworthy of himself. But, as he came closer to them, to his astonishment, he heard them speaking Yiddish, and in a state of disbelief, he realized that they must have been Jews from Poland.

As soon as he returned home, he told me about them. "I thought I had seen just about everything there was to see," he said, "But such Jews as these, I have never seen in my entire life." It was a phenomenon to which they gave no further thought.

There came a day, however, when my father called me to his side. "Listen carefully to me, Margot," he said. "... Under Hitler, I would have died because I was a Jew. Under communism, I will die because I am a human being." He paused and took a deep breath before continuing. "... I don't think I will survive this war; but you are young and strong enough to survive it; and when it is over, you must try to get to Germany because, no matter what happens, the West is still the West; but don't be devastated or surprised if you find no Jews left in Europe, because that is Hitler's aim, to destroy all European Jewry. Nevertheless, here and there some survivors will be left and you must get in touch with them."

"But should there be such a cataclysm, how could anyone survive?" I asked.

My father replied, "When a big storm comes and destroys a whole orchard, you will always find a few trees with some apples that have managed to survive. This is a fluke of nature, and that is why there will be some Jews who have survived."

We continued to live in the village for about eight months. Not long after we left for Kirov, the entire village died from starvation.

We heard that in Kirov, a delegation was formed to help the Polish refugees that were in dire need of food and clothing. This had been arranged by the Americans, the Food Federation or the 'Joint' federation, as it was commonly called.

My father's condition was getting worse, and when we arrived in Kirov to see the Polish delegate, Mr. Fink, he was unable to see us for two days and in the meantime, we needed to find a place to sleep.

In Russia, you weren't able to get a room in a hotel, unless you had a pass saying that you were a party member or were there on official business for the government. But such was communist Russia, that there was nothing you couldn't get on the 'black market' if you had the means.

Now there was a woman, a mistress of a highly placed member of the communist party, that had a large apartment, with four rooms, that, normally disallowed, had been given her by her lover, and in each room there were four beds, and she would charge thirty roubles a night for each bed used, which, in all probability, she shared with her lover. Although this was prohibited, if you were a member of the hierarchy, in Russia, you could get away with anything as long as you hadn't made an enemy that might denounce you to better themselves. In fact the practice was not unusual among high ranking members of the government that were bent on getting away with as much as they could. And so my father and I took two of the beds out of the four that were there in the room.

I found it all very disturbing, what with my father's illness and everything else that was happening in our lives, and speaking to my father in my mother tongue, German, I said, "Just look what is going on here in this, supposedly, Russian communist utopia; terrible, terrible things"

The other two beds that were in a corner of the room were occupied by two Russians; and feeling certain that neither of them would be able to understand a word I said, I paid no attention to them. However, when one of them left the room, the other one approached us and said, "Listen, I am a Jew from Odessa and I understand German because of the Yiddish language, and you are putting yourselves in terrible danger, speaking as you did. Do you know who I am...? I am being sent to Dumbas as a commandant of political unreliables that speak just as you did, and they live for only half a year because they are put to work in the iron mines and the iron eats into their lungs" And then he opened his huge trunk and said, "You see what I have here? Garlic, onions, all this stuff because I too cannot stay there for more than six months or I will get scurvy and they will have to send another one in my place.

"I happen to come from a very religious home, and I feel for you; so I am giving you 1,500 roubles plus half of what I have in my trunk. Now, when I leave, you must never open your mouths again, in German or anything like it, because, the other man is also being sent to a job like mine because we are all party members and he is a Ukrainian and an anti-Semite, and he understands Yiddish because he lived amongst the Jews in the Ukraine

"I can't tell you how nervous I was when I heard you speaking, and how relieved I was when he left the room and I could talk to you before he came back. Now when he returns, you don't know me and I don't know you. We have nothing in common any longer; but remember, never speak in German any more, because there are all kinds of Jews out there, like any other kind of people in the world, who will give you up in a moment; and you are lucky that I am a good Jew, because from what I heard, I could get the biggest promotion if I were to denounce you for what was said."

And so we had been warned, and we were grateful to that man who still had feelings for his fellow Jews; unlike a committed communist, he must have come to realize just how much corruption the system brings with it.

Two days later, we went to see the delegate in charge of the Polish mission, Mr. Fink, who happened to be a Polish Jew, appointed by the temporary Polish government, in England, whose head was general Sikorski, and when he saw us he immediately asked, "What can I do for you?"

"Not for me," replied my father, "I am too sick and must go to a hospital; but for my daughter, who is quite literate, you can give her a job, here at the delegation."

Seeing, for himself, how bad the situation was, and being a man of importance, he immediately got in touch with the hospital and arranged for my father to be admitted.

He then arranged a job for me, which entailed receiving the Polish citizens that arrived from all different kinds of gulags from across Russia, and giving them food, clothes and shelter over night before they moved on. Also, after registering them, I would report to the office, how many had arrived that day so that they would know how many had been cared for, and what would be needed for those that were expected to arrive daily.

The 'Joint' wasn't merely for Jewish refugees, but for all Polish citizens who, in the main, were honest and deserving. Unfortunately there are always some who think and feel differently, and one day, such Polish citizens entered the hall in search of food and clothing, and when they saw me, they cried out in bitterness, "Look at them! She's a Jew and the delegate is a Jew, and we have to share with them what we get from the Polish delegation. It's not right! And it's not right that they should be the one's handing it out to us!"

We had all suffered together, Jew and non-Jew alike, and horrified by such an outburst, I ran to tell the delegate in charge what was happening.

Immediately, he picked up a few of the parcels, went down into the hall and threw them at the feet of the complaining refugees, and breaking open the parcels, pulled out the clothes inside and shoved them under their noses. "See who sent these?" pointing to the names on the labels, "Look at them," he ordered, "Goldblatt, a Jew, Greenfeld. a Jew, Rubenstein, a Jew; all the goodies, the clothes, the food, the medicines have been sent by American Jews, everything that you are getting, comes from Jews. Certainly this is a Polish delegation, but it's the Jews who are sending what is needed over from America."

Their argument destroyed, they now understood that what they were getting was because of Jewish charity...! Quietly, they returned to their seats and, looking somewhat uncomfortable, they uttered not another word.

I visited my father in hospital every day after work. It was a harrowing experience. One day, I arrived at the hospital to find that he was no longer there. He had died in the night, they said. All at once, I recalled what he had told to me, just days before 'One day you will come and I will no longer be here. They will kill me. Wounded soldiers are coming back from the front line and they will need the beds.' So it came as no surprise to hear that he was gone. As it was, for days, I watched as he grew thinner and weaker, becoming a shadow of the man I used to know.

When I asked to see him, I was told that he had already been buried along with others who had died during the night. The war was still raging, and there was no time for formal burials, they explained.

I was despondent and tired, too tired even for sorrow and accepted the explanation without question or a word of reproach; I simply turned around and, with one heavy step following the other, trudged out of the hospital and down the front steps into the street, my heart an empty shell. There had been so much tragedy in our lives, it was as if I was no longer human, but a machine that grinds on and on without thought or feeling, doing what I had to do to survive, and right then, survival was uppermost in my mind.

That is how it was, how it always is. When life becomes too unbearable, we draw a veil between that part of our brain that is too painful, and the rest of it that lives on in its shadow, making the most of what is left to us. We are only human, after all, with all the frailties that go with it, and if we still have the want to go on hoping when it seems there is no hope, then that is one of God's greatest gifts to humankind!

Soon after the death of my father, the delegate was taken away by the Russians and imprisoned.

Stalin had decided that the Polish delegation was not trustworthy because they were supported by the temporary Polish government in England. He wanted to have a Polish delegation that was supported by his own government because he already had in mind to begin the takeover of Poland, after the war, and have the necessary people in place that would be able to carry out his plans. And so they put in a Polish delegate who was a communist before the war, and the whole nature of the program changed. There were no more clothes or food relief for the needy; there was just a delegation under the auspices of the Russian communist party to re-educate the people to become good Polish citizens under communism in Poland.

While working for the original delegation, Mr. Fink allowed me to take first pick from the many parcels of clothes that were being sent over by the Americans, hence, I was, in all probability, one of the best dressed young women in the city, and on that day, when those working for the delegation were being led away by the Russian authorities, I was walking to work, dressed in my finery, as usual, when to my surprise I saw a crowd of people, that usually came for help from the delegation, gathered together on the sidewalk outside the building.

No sooner did they see me coming, than they began making gestures with their hands, in an effort to stop me from coming further and to go back as quickly as I could. My heart lurched, something was terribly wrong, and I immediately turned back and went straight home to the apartment I shared with a very nice Russian woman and her daughter.

Since being interned in a gulag, I had no passport, only a document that gave me the right to remain free. But now things had changed, and with those of the delegation having been led away to prison, I feared that it would happen to me and I was too scared to venture out in the open. Firstly because the document restricted me from doing any other kind of work. Secondly, I wasn't even able to get a loaf of bread without the proper papers.

But how long can one be cooped up without going out into the air? And one night, I took a chance and went out for a stroll. Whilst walking, two men, that came out from the shadows, grabbed me saying they came from the government and that I had to go with them; and they took me to an office building that appeared to be some sort of police station, that was set amongst the fields where tomatoes and cucumbers, and other vegetables, were being grown.

It so happened, that this building was across the way from where I worked for the delegation; and the man in charge, an NKVD. had seen me, dressed well and looking very lovely, in my beautiful clothes, from his window, where he also saw what happened to the delegation, after which, he planned to have me picked up and taken to him.

Whilst sitting there, frightened and bewildered by what had happened, this man emerged from one of the offices and said to me, "You come here," and he took me to an office where, the light was so dim that I could barely see where I *was*, and told me that he knew I worked for the delegation, and that I should have been arrested with the others but, somehow had avoided capture and so I must be a spy, or how else could I have escaped.

Trembling with fear, I vehemently protested, "I am not a spy, I am not!"

His eyes narrowing, he said, "Look, I know you are a spy... But... I will tell you something. I will not give you up to the authorities, and for that, you will have sex with me, or else...!"

Still trembling and terrified, even before he said what he did, I was thinking that my life was over and I was going to jail, never to get out and be able to return to the Europe I once knew and loved. But... when he made that sexual advance towards me, it was as if I was hit by a bolt of lightning, and somehow I realized that by saying what he did, he had actually set me free because, in that split second, I recalled a movie that I had seen when young. I couldn't remember its name, but I did remember the plot, and the scene that stood out most was one that was exactly like the situation I was in, at that moment, and from that scene, I knew what had to be done, attack the attacker who was nothing more than piece of garbage, trying it on with me and not an NKVD. as he would have me believe.

And with relief, from this feeling of freedom, I began laughing with hysteria.

His anger rising at the sight of my hysteria, he said, "Why are you laughing like that?"

Calming down, I looked him straight in the eye, and said, "Because now I know that this is a set up. If you are such a good patriot, an NKVD, how come you would let a spy go free for sex? So I will tell you something. I don't mind going to the NKVD.; you can take me there, and I will tell them of your proposition, telling me that I was a spy, but I could go free if I had sex with you; and then you will be the one that goes to jail, not I."

He had been crippled during the war and walked with a cane; and mad with fury, he lifted his cane and began banging his desk with it. Meanwhile, seizing my chance, I jumped up and started to run, and when he ran after me, I swiftly made for the door, opened it and ran out into the hall.

Sitting out there was a Russian woman whose job it was to stay near the door where she heard and saw everything that went on. When I came out, she said to me. "You are a very sophisticated young woman. You are not like the local girls. You are the only one that got out of his office without being sexually molested by him. He does it with everybody. The girls are afraid of him because they steal a little something and he looks for those girls and holds it over them and blackmails them into giving him sex. Sometimes he makes up a story of them stealing, and they are too afraid to deny it, so he gets away with it."

Being of an inquisitive nature, I then discovered that his was a more important job than first realized; beneath those vegetable fields was a network of tunnels where items of war were being stored for which he was responsible. I also found out that he was a married man with children, and that he was most certainly a sexual pervert.

After that incident, I returned to the apartment I lived in with the Russian woman and her daughter. They didn't have much food, but gave me whatever they did have. But with my mind in the state it was, I had a big problem. I had already been thinking that perhaps I would commit suicide and leave behind all the battle and strife that my life had become.

But, as fate would have it, one day whilst out walking, I met, on the street, a Jewish, Polish, man that said to me, "You know, there is a new law, and all Polish citizens are being taken to, what they call 'better places". And so, I went to the new Polish delegation that was under the auspices of the Russian government, and that were taking care of the matter, and told them I was Polish from before the war, and so I was put on a train and taken to 'better places' that was a SOVCHOS.

Under this new scheme, they transported the Polish citizens to a collective farm near the city of Voronezh that was a part of 'Better Places'. Polish citizens from all over Russia, were being sent to such farms, where they could enjoy a better existence and I was sent to a large agricultural village that was under the control of the government, the main crops being potatoes and corn, and everyone there worked for them.

While I was being transported to the, so called, 'Better Places', a gentleman from the Ukraine, who noticed that I was on my own, advised me to go to the Polish woman, whose three daughters I had become friendly with, and tell her that if she told the Russian authorities that I was a fourth daughter of hers, I would be safe from the Russian authorities that would otherwise place me in a barrack for single men and women where I would be repeatedly raped so that my life would no longer be worth anything.

At once, I understood what he was telling me and was grateful for both his kindness and caring and, without a second thought, I sought out the Polish woman, and after explaining, to her, what the man from the Ukraine had told me, she took me in as one of the family.

They were good, decent, people who were very nice to me; but they were all women, there were no men to do the heavy work, and so it was left to us to chop wood for the stove that not only kept the one room we lived in warm but to cook the food that we managed to gather to help keep hunger from our door. We also had to fetch our water from a well that was some distance from our home.

As well, we had to work in the fields, alongside eight hundred others that were working for 'SOVCHOS ' which was a collective farm run by the government to harvest potatoes and all sorts of other vegetables that were then given to the government, leaving almost nothing for ourselves.

While I was walking to the fields, one day, I was approached by a man. "Look here," he said. "I am Jewish and me and my family have just arrived amongst a transport of new people along with another Jewish family of tailors and shoemakers. Now they will give us a larger room if we had just one more person to share it with us; and that could be you. I have seen how hard you have been working, chopping wood and fetching water, and I can save you from this work that can end in a calamity that may lead to death. So if you want to come with us, you will save yourself from these terrible chores. I have three healthy sons to do the hard work with me. My wife and my daughter do not have to work,

Neither will you if you move in with us."

Now exhausted from the work I was doing, the thought of not having to break my back any longer, was tempting; and so I was more than relieved to move in with them and they made a corner of the large room for me, separating it from the rest of the family with a curtain that was hung over a line for privacy, whilst the rest of them slept in beds, that were placed around the room, or on the floor. There was also a stove in a corner on which to cook and prepare the food, little as it was, that was brought into the house from the fields where they worked.

As I continued living with them, I realized that nothing was as it was in a normal family. By day the men worked in the fields like everyone else, but at night they were away, busy with whatever it was they were doing. Try as I did, I couldn't make out what that was, but me, with my enquiring mind, had to find out; so I took the bull by the horns, and dared to ask the father about their activities during the night.

He was neither shy nor ashamed of what he did to make a living. To him it was a business like any other legitimate venture; one that he was born to, you might say, coming from a long line of thieves going back to his grandfather. And this is what he told me - "Before the war, in Poland, we were horse thieves; that is how we made a living. We are now carrying on the tradition of being thieves; if no longer of horses, then of other valuable items that are to be found and stolen."

While he was speaking, it suddenly dawned on me, that these were the same people that my father had told me about when he returned from the black-market place near our village, so many months ago – a lifetime ago, it seemed.

Now to explain this strange family, it must be told that the father was the most normal of them all, despite a crooked mouth that showed a set of crooked teeth that gave him the appearance of a fiend. Now the wife, a tall, ugly woman with the darting eyes of a bird of prey, and a huge growth on her stomach that looked as if the devil himself was inside her, about to be born, was a morose specimen of a witch that had lost her broomstick. Neither did she ever wash; she was filthy from head to toe, with matted hair that smelled of rotting cabbage.

The oldest son, if not simple, was not as bright as his father. Then there was Josh, whose hormones, somehow, became mixed up before he was born, and he appeared to be neither man, nor woman, simply a poor wretch of a boy as he was referred to. While Mendel had a disorder that made him unable to remain still, shaking backwards and forwards, moving his arms and hands up and down, continuously. The only one of the children that was normal, was their daughter, a beautiful girl that they spoiled like a princess, stealing only the best they could find, to give her.

Now the eldest son fell in love with a Russian woman and moved away so that he could be with her. But, as I mentioned, not being as smart as his father, he got caught and was sent to a gulag.

With all this, that was going on, I, being of an open mind like my father, only felt grateful to them for having taken me in as one of the family. My choices were limited and in my heart, I knew what my father would have said to me, 'These are extraordinary times and you have to do the best you can', and living with them was the best I could do.

Now, I had worked in many places, in the 'SOVCHOS' and at that time I worked in a place where the women were bringing in the corn from the fields and filling sacks with it, for distribution to the government.

There were many Russian women working there. It was hard work, but I was strong and worked beside them with pride and not let any of those I worked with, help me; and they said to me. "You know, you're not like a Jewish girl, you are a hard worker."

I liked the women and didn't take offence; I understood that they couldn't help the way they thought. They had been brain washed by the Greek orthodox priests who told them that Jews were lazy and that they would use other people to do the work for them, so I said to them, "Listen, you are being very prejudiced against my people. My being who I am is not because I am Jewish or not Jewish. This is the way I am, a human being, and there are all kinds of Jews, just like there are all kinds of any other people." Then they were sorry for what they had said and never made such a remark again.

Another time they told me how much they liked me and how sorry they were for me because of Hitler and what would happen to me when the Germans came. So I said to them, "While you feel sorry for me, you might as well feel very sorry for yourselves, because Hitler doesn't like the Slavs and thinks of them as subhuman and injects them with a monkey serum to make them work as automats for the Aryan race, and he treats the Russian soldiers like animals, and you should know that in heading for Moscow, he had many Russian peasants killed along the way. All the Russian peasants, he killed. So don't feel pity for me, it's better you be well informed and have pity on yourselves, because Hitler is a perverted maniac and he is no good for anybody!"

Anyhow, going back to the sacks of corn, in those harsh days of hunger and strife, if you didn't steal, even the smallest amount from whatever was available to eat, you starved. It was risky, but when the alternative was an empty belly, you took that risk, and everyone was doing it.

I would take handfuls of the corn from the sacks and hide them in one of the pockets under my jacket; I would then bring home the corn to cook and eat, hiding it, meanwhile, in a dish that I kept under my bed in the belief that it would be safe; Not so, every time I went to take it out to cook, it had disappeared. Realizing that it had to be the wife who must have seen me putting it under the bed – many times I witnessed her stealing little things from all over the village and the 'SOVCHOS', as did her husband – I felt I had to do something about it.

But I was scared, and couldn't sleep at night, frightened to close my eyes for fear of what else she might steal from me; not that I had anything of value to steal; but that is what the woman did as naturally as breathing air.

Her husband knew, very well, that his wife was stealing; so what was the point of telling him what his wife was doing, I decided. But I had to come up with something to tell him, so that he would stop his wife from taking from me.

After much thought, it came to me, when I recalled a story that my father had told me; that in the town where he was born, there was a very rich man whose wife suffered from kleptomania, she couldn't help stealing from the stores she entered. Not wanting her to be prosecuted for theft, her husband made a deal with the storekeepers. They would allow her to take whatever she wanted, and they would keep a record of it and present her husband with the total cost of the items at the end of each week.

No sooner had the story come to mind, I knew what had to be done. I had to bolster the man's ego by comparing him to that rich man; and when I found him alone, one day, I struck.

I related the story of the very rich man whose wife was a kleptomaniac. "You know, Mr. Kay," I said, "I think your wife has the same sickness as that very rich, intelligent and highly educated woman because she is stealing from me. She takes, from under my bed, the corn that I put there to cook and eat because I am very hungry."

"Hmmm!" he murmured, "You know, I have a great regard for you. You did not go out and tell the other Jewish family about this, because I look up to them and I wouldn't want them to know that may wife even steals from you. So you are not only smart but a very nice, good girl."

As he said this to me, his wife came in and he said to her, "You see this," and he pointed to the leather belt that held up his pants, "If you dare to take anything from her, from under her bed, you will feel this belt on you. And what's more, not only do you not take it from her, but you will cook it for her so that when she comes home, she will have a warm meal to eat."

The wife knew that it was nothing more than an act, by her husband, so she feigned obedience, "Okay! Okay! Enough, enough already," she cried, and that was the end of that.

A few days later, the husband came to me and said, "They have opened up a Polish delegation in the city of Voronezh, and I am going there with my sons and you can come with us too. They are giving away big parcels of clothes and food, it's worth a fortune, and you can go with us if you want to go."

I was quick to respond. "Yeah!" I said, "I would love to go, but how can I get on the train, because in Russia, to get on the train is almost impossible?"

"You leave that to me because, the conductor is bought off. I do all sorts of things with the conductor, so don't you worry about going on the train," he said.

So I went with him and his sons on the train that looked more like a cattle car than a passenger train. It was night, and it was pitch black out, and the Russian peasants were lying on the wooden seats and on the floors, wherever they could find a space. And the Russian women would come with their sacks of bread that they had baked to sell in the city, and place them beneath their heads to sleep on, as they didn't trust everyone or anyone that was sleeping on the train; and you would have to be a Houdini to steal bread away from them.

It was late at night, and having reached its destination, the train was slowing down, when, all of a sudden, I heard Josh saying in Yiddish, ' Dad', and somehow it struck me that he was stealing, and that the word 'Dad' was a signal. So swiftly I rose from my hard bench, and followed him and his family, along the train. Somehow, they had managed to steal the bread from beneath the Russian woman's head, and as I suspected, the word 'dad' was a signal to run. So, without another thought, and with my heart pumping wildly, I rushed after them. The train had just stopped, and they jumped, and then gave me a hand to jump down with them.

In the meantime, the Russian woman was screaming, "Thieves, thieves, stop them." And the police that always accompanied the train, started running after us.

Darkness surrounded us like a thick blanket, and I started running with them– fast, faster, faster still, my legs bounding over the unseen, shadowy ground, like the legs of an animal running in fear of a predator. For miles we ran until, the father, suddenly stopping, said, "Now we have no need to run any further and can relax. No one is following us anymore."

Gasping for breath, we sat down, and the father took out a knife, that he always carried with him, and began cutting up the bread they stole and handed it round.

I was filled with anger, and I said to the father, "Mr. Kay, let us talk a bit. Tell me, what did you achieve by stealing this bread? You put yourself and us in mortal danger, and for what? The war is almost over and we will soon be deported to Poland or somewhere else.... I am very surprised at you because you are a very clever man," I said, building him up. "A clever man like you should have told your sons not to steal from those women."

And he replied, "You know, Margot, when you talk to me like this, I know you are right. We really have more luck than judgement. But I will tell you something else that I never told you before. I may be a thief, but I have a Jewish heart. What did you think, when I asked you to live with us? It wasn't because I wanted a bigger place, I had pity on you.... I knew you were a Jewish girl from a higher social class above us, and that, if it were not for the war, you would never have had anything to do with people like us. But having a Jewish heart, when I saw how hard you were working, I wanted you to come with us so that you could say afterwards, that you survived because of us, and this will be a credit on me."

"Yes!" I said, "You did me a big favour, and one more thing I have to tell you... morally, as far as sexually, is concerned, you really are fine Jewish people." And his face brightened with pleasure.

We then went to the office of the delegation who gave us what we were entitled to, and we returned to 'SOVCHOS'. A few weeks later, we were transported to Poland. In the transport, there were trains that went one way or another, and Mr. Kay found a friend that, in all probability, was a thief like he was, and he asked Kay, "How did you survive in Russia?"

Wanting to raise his standing, he said, "How did I survive in Russia...? I was a king in Russia. You ask this young lady with us and she will tell you."

"Really...?" said the man in surprise, "He was a king? I knew him for a thief...!"

"Oh no!" said I, "He was a king..."

After that, when we reached our destination, we each went our own way and I never saw them again.

In those days, the majority of Poles who came from Russia were not very literate; the intelligentsia being killed off by the Germans and then the Russians. I was considered literate and when the train reached its destination, I was summoned to the office of the commandant, a short, bulky, Russian with a round, ruddy, face and the broad features of a peasant, and he said, "We are going to make here, with the Polish people, a little organisation for the youth of the community, and you will be presiding over them, and we will give you books from which you will read to them."

They gave me no choice in the matter; it was, however, a good job. Even so, the books were full of communist propaganda, Marxism, Leninism, Stalinism, and I soon realized that what they really wanted was for me to tell them what was said, during the readings, knowing that the Poles and the Ukrainians that were there, didn't want any of it, and it would give them the opportunity to send them back to the gulag.

Day after day, I would read to them from the books, and they, being ignorant, would laugh and curse and cry, "Aha! So Hitler was no good, and Stalin is any better!" And they would shrug their shoulders.

Now the Russian communists behind the plan, were very shrewd; they knew that I was Jewish and a Holocaust survivor, and they knew that I would be so mad when I heard them speak favourably of Hitler, that I would report what was being said. But they had found the wrong Jewess; no way was I an informer and especially not for the communists.

I had read the books, and hated every word of their content, and that evening, I went home to the one room that I shared with five others, and didn't sleep a wink for nights because I knew, that there would come a day when the commandant would call me in to his office to question me about the people's reaction to what they were listening to and I would be expected to provide him with a suitable answer and it took many nights for me to consider what my reply would be; and eventually I came to the conclusion that to lie was my only recourse.

"Look!" I said when called before him, "Russia needs people to work; you are wasting your time with these books, they don't listen to a word, they sleep in the class they don't learn anything. Now I am a patriot of Russia because of what you did for us Jews, you went to war for us, and I am telling you, reading to them is a waste of time. Let them work for the Soviet Union."

His steely grey eyes seemed to bore into mine while questioning me...I watched him closely, as he took his time to consider his reply, noticing how the short stubby fingers of his podgy hands kept drumming on the desk top while thinking. All at once they became still and, palms up, shoulders hunched, he made a gesture of hopelessness whilst murmuring, "Hmmm... You are probably right, why should we waste so many hours reading to them when they could be of more use to us in the fields..." Suddenly, his eyes widened with admiration and he said, "You know, you really are a good patriot, a good girl; we need people like you on our side!"

I breathed with relief, I had fooled him...Of course it made me mad when they spoke of Hitler in such a mild way, but one thing had nothing to do with another; I was not one to rat on others, it was not, and never would be my way. There had already been too much suffering in the world, and I was not going to add to it by being an informant.

At the same time as I read the books, I had to work, but they gave me a better job... It also happened that I was at the right place, in a time of shortages...They gave me a large weighing scale for the potatoes when they came in from the fields. There were wet potatoes and dry potatoes that had to be kept in large holes in the ground during the winter months. I had never seen a potato that came straight from the fields, but common sense told me that the wet and dry potatoes should be placed in separate holes else they would all rot.

In that village there were 350 hungry Russian women and their children, whose husbands were on the front line fighting for Russia; and when I started to give the orders for the potatoes to be separated so that there would be enough good potatoes to feed the hungry, in winter, the officer in charge of the operation came up to me and said, "Stop that for a moment and come with me, I need to have a talk with you," and he said, "Did you think I gave you such a cushy position for your beautiful eyes?"

Somewhat confused, I replied "No! I didn't think so, but please, explain yourself because I don't understand what it is that you want?"

"It's like this," he said, "You must put the wet potatoes with the dry, and the dry potatoes with the wet; do that and I will see to it that you have enough food to eat for the entire winter. Now do you understand?"

I was beginning to comprehend the situation and didn't like it one bit. What were those poor women and children going to do? They would surely die of hunger; but then, what choice did I have in the matter? If I didn't do it, somebody else would have. And so I did what I had to do.

Nevertheless, I wasn't the sort of person that could accept something so outrageous without knowing the reason behind it, and so I investigated the situation for myself and found out that those, so called communists, who wielded power over the poor peasants who worked in the fields, were gathering the bad potatoes and giving them to the directors of the local distilleries to make Vodka. And the more bad potatoes they gave them, for which the directors signed, the more money they made, sharing the increased profits with the communist officers. It wasn't only for the money, the officers were given the best food and grew fat, like pigs, and drank vodka, and had orgies, and the peasants were dying whilst they ate well. I was also given enough potatoes and pickles to help me survive the winter And so I spent the remainder of the war doing what was expected of me. It wasn't an easy situation, and then, nothing about the war had been easy for me; but at least I was surviving.

So much for communism...! So much for bureaucracy when unelected government officials had everything and the people in the street had nothing except a spy in their midst to report on what was being said, if anything, against the regime. Even if the people knew something wrong was going on, they had to remain silent or be prepared to take the consequences; which usually meant, Siberia.

While working at SOVCHOS, at one of the many places I was sent to, there came a day when I happened to be sitting in my room without anything to do. Now, in every SOVCHOS or factory in Russia, there were two main directors, amongst many others; one, of whom, was a director of work, while the other was a director of politics who took care of the political situation, and was commonly referred to as a 'politruk'

In that particular SOVCHOS there was a party political commissar, Gindin, that was Jewish and who, before the war was a reporter writing for a paper in the city of Voronezh. Having been injured, during the war, and unable to walk without a cane, he could no longer be in the front line of the fighting.

Now there was a time, in Russia, when a wave of Anti-Semitism was taking a hold of the political establishment and they wanted to get rid of their Jewish colleagues. Gindin was well aware of this and didn't want to lose his position; so he took whatever measures he could think of to save his post, using me to this end. Making it his business to know when I was in my room, he came barging in, one day and abruptly ordered, "You come with me to the office."

Bewildered, having no idea why he wanted me to go with him, and knowing that I had no choice in the matter, I followed him to the office where there must have been about thirty people working as secretaries and accountants doing all kinds of paper work for the SOVCHOS where 800 hundred people needed to be overseen.

Without ceremony, in front of all these people, making certain that everyone should hear what he had to say to me, he yelled, "What kind of a person are you...? Do you know we are spilling our blood in order to win the war against the fascists? And you don't want to work and participate in this important war of our mother country...?"

Quick to realize why he was doing this, I lost my temper and without thinking of the consequences, cried out in Russian "You dirty Jew; you are using me to further your ambitions. You have the nerve to tell me, in front of all these Russian people, that I am some kind of lazy good for nothing, that doesn't want to contribute to the victory of the Russian government. You were in the army and you know, very well, that I am the lone survivor of my entire family. You saw what Hitler did to the Jews, and now you are accusing me of being unpatriotic? You ought to be ashamed of yourself..!"

Furious that I should have turned on him, and that it hadn't worked out the way he planned; as well, seeing that the sympathy of the other workers was with me and not him, he turned red and, trembling with rage, lifted his cane in the air;

but before he had a chance to strike, I began to run from the room with him in hot pursuit, screaming in Russian "I will get you, I will put you in jail for this."

In fear of paying with my life for having spoken up for myself, I ran to another Polish Jew named, Aaron and told him what a serpent Gindin was. Now Aaron happened to be engaged to marry Gindin's sister, an ungainly woman who, but for Aaron, might never have had a chance to marry; and angered by the unjust behaviour of Gindin, and having influence with the family, he immediately ran to Gindin's house and said to him, "If you ever do anything against Margot, I will not marry your sister."

"But why did she have to call me a dirty Jew like that?" said Gindin. "She shamed me!"

"And why did you have to take her to that office and talk to her like that in front of everyone? You shouldn't have done it, and she shouldn't have done it. But with everything that is happening to her, she lost control because she is hurting, and you don' take a person that is hurting and make them a scapegoat for your own selfish purpose"

And so, despite himself, Gindin backed down. As well he didn't want to end up with his sister on his hands.

When the war came to an end, it was summer time, and the people were taken by wagon trains, normally used for cattle, back to Poland. I had proved to be very good with the books I'd been given, as well as with the work I'd been appointed to do; and so I was looked upon, by the party, as good communist material for Poland.

They were sorely in need of such people and, like me, there were many Jews who were semi educated and considered ripe for communism. But, unlike me, who had seen with my own eyes, the Russian cruelty that was as bad as anywhere, including Hitler's Germany; as well, the further up the ladder the communist officials rose, the more decadent they became, some Jews only saw the Russians as liberators from Hitler's reign of terror, and became very pro Russian, and thereby, pro communism.

I was given all the necessary papers, and was told, that when we reached Iignitza, that was part of Germany, before the war and was now part of Poland since the Germans lost the war I was to be a politrook, which meant I would be a political commissar, and would be given a villa to live in that had belonged to a German, and I would be trained for the position before we left. However, I was warned, by the Russians who, uncharacteristically, suddenly become concerned about the Jews, that we had to be careful of those Poles that were going around killing the Jews who had returned to Poland, and that it was going on in small villages all over the country. It wasn't the best of news, but there was nothing I could do about it. Come what may, I knew I had to leave Russia.

On the train with me was another of my faith, a man named, Aaron, who was eleven years older than I, and while he had been a tailor, before the war, he was also highly intelligent and believing him to be a good communist, he was appointed, by the Russian government to be their lackey and do their bidding, as prime minister of Iignitza and the surrounding area.

It was a long journey and that night, when we were no longer moving, they slide back the doors of the enclosed wagons to let in some fresh air, and Aaron and I, with the rest of the Ukrainians and Poles travelling with us, stepped down from the train to stretch our legs.

All at once, I heard a whisper, "Amcho!" I knew this to be Hebrew meaning 'Plain Jewish folk' and somewhat taken aback, in a whisper, I answered, 'Amcho!' and to my surprise, standing in the shadows of the wagon were two tough looking men with machine guns, who were Jewish partisans during the war, and a, Jewish, Palestinian that knew that there were many Jews returning from Russia and was there, as an emissary from Palestine, to find those who wished to go to the Holy Land, and let them know that there was a way to get out of Poland altogether, and enter West Germany, that was under American occupation, and that from there they would be able to decide where they wanted to go. Naturally, they wanted them to go to Palestine, and if not, they wanted to save the remnants of Jewish people from the clutches of communist countries.

When asked what I was doing there, on the train, I told them, "I am here with one other Jew, and we are going to Iignitzia where a very important job with the communist party is waiting for us."

The Palestinian pushed the other two aside and stepped forward. "Look it's like this," he said, "if you want this big job, then do what you must; but there is an opportunity for you to leave Poland altogether. We are here looking for Jews who want to go to Palestine. Now there are two cities, Lodz and Warsaw where you have to go if you want to leave Poland."

My heart quickened. "Yes, yes, I would like to go, but how can I, I have no money for a ticket." I cried.

"We thought of that," he said, "and have prepared money to help pay for the tickets. Now the doors of the train will soon close and, in twenty minutes you will be in Poznan. Go down from the train and go and get yourself a ticket, with the money we give you, to Lodz or Warsaw, whichever city you want; and there, you will sit on a bench, at the station, and someone will pass by and say 'Amcho', and you must reply, 'Amcho', and then this person will take you to a place where there are a lot of young Jews who survived the war, and who are now a part of a Zionist organisation."

I couldn't believe my ears, I was so happy, so overjoyed and cried out, "Okay! Okay! Give me the money, and give me enough for the Jewish guy with me. Come on; come on before it leaves."

I returned to the train; impatiently, waiting for the doors to close, and the moment we began rolling, I went over to Aaron, and breathless with excitement, gasped, "...You know what happened! You know what happened...! It's unbelievable!" and I told him the whole story.

He scoffed, and said, "... You know, you really are stupid. Such a wonderful position is waiting for you and me, and you want to sacrifice everything by leaving, and leaving for where and for what!"

"... Oh my God!" I cried in disbelief. "You know what they say in Russian? 'On somebody's bread, don't open your mouth'. Poland is not our country, and as soon as the Russians find Polish communists to put in our place, we will have no rights and will be sent to Siberia; you can't trust them. So let the Poles do their own shit!"

"That may be how you think, but I don't."

"Okay! Have it your way," I said, "but I no longer want to discuss communism with you, the Russians or anyone else, it's not for me! I only did what I had to do because I had no choice."

"Then you go, I'm staying," he said

I heaved a sigh of frustration; I couldn't understand how someone, who had lived with communism for so long, knowing that everyone was spying on everyone else. How could he be so stupid? Was he that hungry for power he would give up his freedom just to rule over other helpless people? ...

I was sorely disappointed by his attitude... He was no better than a rabbit hiding in a field, trying its best not to be noticed by the hunters.

Anyhow, he meant nothing to me except for the fact that he was a Jew, and so, twenty minutes later, I left the train at Poznan, and bought a one way ticket, for myself, to Lodz... All I had with me was a small valise in which there was a dress. In those days, it was a big deal for me to have a dress to wear and I planned to wear it when I got there, so that I would look like a normal human being and not as if I had just arrived from the backwoods. But I didn't dare wear it yet, for fear of spoiling it before I got there.

When the train arrived, clutching, tightly, my little valise that held the precious dress, I got into one of the compartments and sat down, holding the case close to me. Half sitting half flopping in their seats across the aisle from me were two, coarse looking, drunken Russian soldiers with wide faces and short cropped hair, laughing and making vulgar jokes that, I, fluent in Russian, understood and, an elderly, well mannered, Polish, gentleman with grey hair, worn longer than the current fashion and, elegantly brushed back over his ears like a musician or professor, a well groomed, grey, moustache and a pair of fine, light brown, eyes beneath well defined grey eyebrows, whom I recognised at once as being of a noble class of person.

Watching my every move, as I sat quietly in a corner of the carriage, their small, beady, eyes half closed from too much booze, the nauseating smell of liquor on their breath drifting towards me, one of the soldiers suddenly said, his slurred speech rolling the short sentence into one, flat sounding, word, "Gimmeyourvalise."

Having come from Russia, I understood, that in those days, no matter how bad things were, you didn't behave in that way, or you would be put in a gulag for criminals. But these two soldiers wanted as much vodka as they could get and I knew that they would exchange the valise and its contents for it; and so, hooking my arm over the valise, drawing it protectively closer to me, I began to argue with them in Russian.

They glanced slyly at one another and then the other one said, his delivery somewhat more coherent, "If you don't give it to us, we'll throw you out of the window!"

As yet, it still hadn't sunk in to my head that it was after the war and the Russians were now part of the new order and could do, very much, as they pleased.

The elderly gentleman, who was sitting quietly by, noted my reluctance to give in, and fearing the worst, bent slightly towards me murmuring in Polish, "Listen, miss, this is no longer a normal country but an occupied one with no law and order. These soldiers will do exactly as they said; you have been through hell to survive, and if you want to continue to live, you had better leave them the valise and get out of here as fast as you can."

It took but a split second to comprehend what he was telling me- I was playing with my life. They were now the masters and, to top it all, they were drunk and would have no compunction in doing whatever it took to get what they wanted, and would have had fun doing it... After everything, it was so unfair; but that's how it was...! All at once my heart began pounding, pounding, pounding like crazy and, without another thought, I rose, left the valise, with its precious content, behind on the seat, and swift as an arrow, pushed back the sliding door to the compartment, slipping through the opening even before it had time to fully extend itself, and ran along the corridor, to the other end of the train, as fast as my feet would carry me. My life had been filled with troubles; I couldn't take any more, I'd had enough!

I had chosen Lodz as the city I wanted to go to. I had family there, and knew it well. When we arrived at the station, I stepped down from the train and, with a strong sense of expectation, sat down on a bench, as I was told to do, and waited, feeling like a poor little orphan who had just come in from the storm, and had nothing to wear but the dowdy dress that I'd been wearing forever, so it seemed.

Sitting on the edge of the bench, my breathing heavy my shoulders tense, I kept looking, searchingly, at every man that passed, all the time wondering if this was the one or that was the one. At long last, a man walked stealthily past whispering, "Amcho!"

Heart in mouth, I replied, "Amcho!"

"Follow me," he said and without another word, walked ahead in front of me.

Immediately rising to my feet, I followed him through street after street, until we came to an apartment building and, upon entering, I followed him up the stairs to a huge apartment, where there were a number of young people, twenty girls and forty boys to be exact, who were gathered together in one place with the purpose of getting out of Poland; as well, to protect each other from those Poles that would attack Jewish people. Some of the leaders, of the group were equipped with guns in case of such an emergency.

These illegal organizations were, in all probability, known by the Russians who were well aware of all that went on in the city, but it was soon after the war and everything was in disarray and they had more than enough on their plate to deal with, so they were not disposed to do anything about them.

I knew Lodz very well, and when the man, who took me to the apartment, mentioned the name of the street where it was situated it rang a bell; but why, I wasn't certain until I entered the sumptuous accommodation and immediately knew that I had been there before.

My mother had a very rich aunt who lived in Lodz in one of the larger apartments in the city and, by a fluke, I was now standing in those familiar surroundings, my mind going back, in time, to how beautiful it had been, and for the first time in ages, I experienced a pang for all that once was and now lost forever.

I didn't mention it to anyone. What was the point? It was so huge and grand, being big enough to comfortably lodge so many, that they probably wouldn't have believed me anyhow.

Amongst them was a Jewish fellow, a Polish citizen, who called himself Fritz. The moment I heard his name, something snapped inside me. It wasn't a name that an upper class German would think of calling himself; it was a name used mostly by the lower classes. But having been considered sub human, for so many years, by the Germans, I believed that he must have lost his sense of dignity and gave himself a name that, somehow, made him more comfortable with himself. Still, for whatever reason, it made me angry and I cringed at the thought that he might have felt that way.

He was the eldest person there, tall, thin, with a sallow complexion and rimless glasses, a typical intellectual type that was probably appointed by one of the left wing Zionist organizations to be their spokesperson. To me, all intellectual leftists were idiots who hid their head in the sand and didn't understand the ideology behind communism, and that it could not apply itself to human nature because human beings are not animals, they are a diverse species with individual thoughts and feelings and it wasn't natural for them to be contained. They need expression which communism denies them while speaking of equality that never was and never would be achieved under such a system, especially where those in office lived on top of the world, while the rest of the people were kept at the bottom of the pile, with no right of free speech, movement or to question. It is fascism at its extreme. And so, when I was introduced to him, with frustration welling up inside me I cried. "What kind of a business is this? Fritz! Where are you a Fritz from?"

I had been living on the edge for so long that all those pent up feelings, all my concealed emotions came flooding out, and I really let him have it, calling him a fool, and a ne'er do well, amongst other unpleasant things, while the rest looked on in astonishment.

However, nothing I said appeared to register, and as if he hadn't heard a word I said, he asked, "Are you a leftist?" His tone sounding as if it was something to be proud of.

Somewhat calmer, I gave him a long hard look!

It so happened, that when I was picked up by the man at the station, he told me that he was from a left-wing organization, but if I preferred, I could wait for another who was from a different Zionist group to come by, and I could go with them.

I didn't have to think about it, and swiftly replied, "Yes! I will go with you." But I didn't give him the reason why; and when I came to the apartment and the man called Fritz inferred that if I came to them, I must be a leftist, I saw red and burst out, "You should be ashamed of yourself. I came to the leftists because I understood that you are getting better food and lodging from the government because they like you; and this is why I came to you. But a Jew is a Jew, is a Jew and should not be one way or the other; we should be for each other after the terrible war we have all gone through. I am no leftist and never will be; I am here for the goodies and only the goodies; you just remember that!"

He stared at me in confusion, uncertain how to respond; and then, shaking his head, he said "Alright! Alright!" and took me to the room where the girls were staying.

In those days, morality was very high and the girls were separated from the boys, and there was never anything that might be considered provocative going on between them, even though there were couples who liked each other very much and knew that, one day, they would marry and settle down together, they never dreamed of doing anything that their late, parents would not have approved of before that all important wedding night.

When I came into the room where the rest of the girls were, they asked my name.

"Margot...!" I said. "Look, I have been travelling for some time and I'm very tired, so if you will excuse me, I would like to get some sleep now."

There were nineteen girls and I was the twentieth. No one had very much, whatever we did have we were wearing to cover our bones. That's all most of us were, a bag of bones from having little to eat during the war. As soon as I was directed to the last vacant bed, I crawled in between the covers, laid my head on the pillow and closed my eyes. I was even more tired than I realized, but my head was swimming with all sorts of thoughts that made sleep impossible.

The others were huddled in a corner of the room, listening to one of the girls who was speaking in a low tone; nevertheless, I heard every word. "I know this girl," she whispered, "She was originally from Germany, and was in the same school and same class with me, where I spent three months. I didn't recognise her at first, she was so beautiful then, so well groomed and we all looked up to her. But I remember that she had a space between her two front teeth, and when she said her name was

Margot, and I saw the same space between her teeth, I knew, at once, that it was her."

When I heard this, my pulse began to race; it seemed like a miracle to me. During the war, the Jews had become as bits of straw blown in the wind and scattered far and wide, far, far away from everything that they knew and would never know again; now, to hear that I was still remembered as I once was, it was as if a door, to which I had lost the key, suddenly opened and, jumping off the bed, I ran over to the girl with excitement, "Yes, yes," I cried, "I went to that school, *and* I was in that class… I can't tell you how good it makes me feel that, at least, one person remembers me from before the war." And if a tear glistened in my eye, then it was the first for many, many a year.

I learned that we were to be smuggled into East Berlin that was under Russian jurisdiction, and that we would be travelling with false papers as German Jews that were allowed to return to Germany. There must have been thousands of Jews who were being smuggled out in that way, few of whom were actually of German origin; and so I realized that there had to be bribery on a big scale if the Russian officials turned a blind eye and allowed Zionist groups to operate out of Poland and send so many young people to Germany.

I was there, in that apartment, for six weeks before I was chosen, with a group, to be smuggled into East Berlin, as German Jews.

While waiting, I decided to take a look around Lodz, where many of my father's relatives had lived, before the war. As I looked around, tears fell from my eyes,, it was as though I was walking through a cemetery instead of the bustling, alive city, that my father always spoke of, full of energy with the sound of laughter and conversation at every street corner. It was the second largest city in Poland, as well as the largest industrial city that exported their textiles all over the world. Now it was completely dead with no life, nothing. I was choking with the thought of all my father's relatives that had been murdered by the Nazi killing machine. It was too much to bear, and so I turned around to go back to the apartment where I was hiding.

While walking back, I heard my name being called, and turning to see who it was, I couldn't believe my eyes, it was Wagner. After we embraced he wanted to know how come I was there, and what happened to me and my father during the war? When I explained what happened and what I was doing there. He became very serious. "You don't want to go to Palestine, you will have a hard life there; you have already been through so much. Go to Germany, meet a nice young man, get married and go with him to America," he said. "… You know, I have your father to thank for my life. After he was picked up by the police, I knew that it was time for me to run away. You see, I was doing so well, that I would have stayed on and on until I got caught. But because I knew your father so well, I ran and escaped into deepest Russia, and there I survived the war."

Before we parted, once again, he said. "Remember, go to Germany, not Palestine."

It made me recall my father telling me that after the war, I was to go to Germany, 'The west will always be the west,' he said. Now Wagner was saying something similar. And with the faintest of smiles, I replied, "I will!"

At that time, there were many barges, belonging to German businessmen, that carried raw materials, back and forth, between Stettin and East Germany, and they were bribed by the Zionists to carry these groups into Germany for them. The man organizing the escape was a Palestinian Jew, and when he came to the apartment to explain the situation, he asked, "Is there anyone amongst you that can speak a good German?"

"I speak German, a Berliner German," I said.

"That's good," he said, "because should there be an inspection of the barge, you, and you alone, will go on deck before they have a chance to go down into the hold, where you will all be hiding, and speak to them in German in the hope that they will not look any further. But remember, only you, not anyone else! Is that clear?"

We all agreed and were then taken, by night to where the barge was moored, and smuggled aboard.

Sure enough, there was one amongst us, a Russian Jew, who had spent his early years in and out of prison since the age of fourteen, when he lost his parents and not knowing what happened to them, to survive, he dealt in the black market and was continually being picked up by the police and put away where he mixed with the most hardened of criminals.

He became, what is termed as 'a jailbird' with the arched eye brows that the male prisoners sported to give them a sinister appearance. Yet, to the contrary, as big and strapping as he was, he was a gentle and kind person, and amazingly simple for one who was used to mixing with the toughest of the underworld. He did, however, have some strange mannerisms, not that they were particularly feminine or masculine, but there was an element of femininity about them. Heaven knows what went on in those prisons, but whatever did happen or didn't they were his secret and his alone.

His greatest fault was that he couldn't accept orders, they reminded him of prison where he had suffered authority, day in day out and had to obey the jailors who would come down hard on him if he didn't do as he was told. Now that he had freedom of choice, he chose to ignore those in command and do exactly as he pleased.

That he ended up in Lodz was by chance. The Russians had a habit of taking the male prisoners and putting them on the front line of a fight; in Vanka's case, it was against the Germans around Warsaw and when he realized that he was in danger of losing his life, he deserted, and under fire ran away, to the city in search of others, of the Jewish faith, in whom he could trust.

He came across many and when he told them his story, they decided that he would have to be hidden because he was in more danger than any of them and they took him to the Zionist group that he was now with.

Everyone liked Vanka, and he liked everyone, especially Sonja, who had lost an arm fighting with a segment of Jewish partisans, blowing up bridges, mining roads and railway tracks where trainloads of Jews were being shipped to death camps all over the country.

And so Vanka, with his easy going manner and lack of discipline, defied authority and went on deck whilst the barge was on route to East Germany and began whistling a Russian tune.

The Brichah should have warned them, that beside the German who owns the barge, a Russian secret policeman would be sitting, spying on him to report anything that wasn't as it was supposed to be. When he heard the whistling, he knew that something was wrong. Russians didn't run away to go to East Germany, so he called to Vanka, "Hey Tovaritch?"

Vanka lost his bearings, and without thinking, in a jovial manner, replied in Russian.

The Russian spy's eyes narrowed with suspicion, "How is it that you are on this barge? You are a Russian, why would a Russian want to go to Germany? he asked

It was then that it hit Vanka. He had made a terrible mistake, and not knowing what else to do, he just stood there, and shrugged.

Immediately, the Russian ordered the German to stop the barge and call the police.

I, to my horror, witnessed all that whilst on deck, went back down into the hold and told the others what to expect.

It was unbelievable! They were so close to freedom… Beside themselves with disappointment, they settled down and waited for the police who were quick in arriving to take them back to Lodz.

No one blamed Vanka, he was what he was, just a simple guy who had nothing but goodness in his heart.

The Russian secret police realized that they were illegally there, and that they were not German, as they were led to believe, and put them all in jail. Meanwhile, the German who owned the barge, got in touch with the Zionist organization, and told them what had happened.

The 'Joint' then got in touch with those whom they knew were open to bribery, and paid them enough, for each one of us, to be set free, after which we were taken, by the Brichah, who were a Palestinian unit formed by the Jewish Brigade, that had, once, been attached to the British army, and the Hagganah, one of the groups fighting for the establishment of a Jewish state, were used by the Zionists to carry illegally those Jews wishing to go to West Berlin, to Stettin from where they would be smuggled out again, to where they wanted to go.

That was only one of the routes the Brichah used to transport, illegally, those Jews who wished to leave Poland – Italy and Austria, amongst others, were also used. But that particular group were directed through Berlin.

At that time, things in Berlin were chaotic; people were running from East to West, and from West to East in droves, according to what they believed would be in their best interest, democracy or communism. No dividing line had been established yet, or what part of Berlin belonged to who; the Wall didn't exist as yet and passage between the two sectors was, basically, unobstructed.

As well, at that time a movement was going on, by the Germans, under the occupational force, to help with the situation, and temporary detention centres, were set up to deal with those Germans who were running from East to West and were believed to be of German nationality.

West Berlin was under occupation by the American and Russian armies, and the Red Cross were helping to organize the stream of migration of the people. The Zionist groups took advantage of the situation, giving Jewish immigrants, false papers that declared they were of German nationality and placed them together, at the detention centres, where our group were given a large room, at a centre, that was not, as yet, under Russian jurisdiction, but under the Red Cross. We were also advised to mingle, as German Jews, with the German people who were going from East Berlin to West Berlin.

The Soviet secret police were distrusting of everyone and everything and I was certain, that the man, who sat outside the door, was really there to spy on us and report back anything that he heard that was unusual.

What he reported confirmed their suspicions; no German was spoken, only Polish, Russian and Yiddish, amongst other languages. But they had to be careful, they had no authority over us, and so they sent in one of their officers to talk to us and trick us into giving ourselves away, which would give them the right to send us back to the East, because they were spying on us and already knew that we were not German Jews as we were supposed to be.

Nevertheless, the Soviet secret police were guarded, and asked to talk to a representative who could speak on the groups behalf.

Amongst us was a young man of 29 who had lived in Russia for many years but, somehow, remained naive and completely ignorant of the Soviet's deceitful politics, and it was this man that the Russian chose to speak for us, and took him to meet their commander.

I was uneasy, I didn't trust the Russians and knew that, somehow, they would corner that simpleton into giving away our main purpose for being there; but there was nothing that could be done about it; he had been chosen and it was now in the hands of the 'Gods' and I waited with bated breath, for his return.

He came back, all excited, believing that he had done well for everyone. "The Russian was wonderful and so understanding of our position," he exclaimed with satisfaction, "'Tomorrow', he told me ' is when we leave here to go to the West; but it's a long way, so why would you want to walk when we can provide transport for you,' he said, ' and that he had already laid on busses to take us to the West. So what do you say?' he asked me.

"Of course I agreed at once," he said, thinking himself smart. "All I had to do was put my signature to the order form for transport to be provided to take us where we want to go."

When I heard this, I became hysterical. "Since when did the Russians care about anybody? Why would they care if we walk or ride? They took you in! They have found us, now they are going to send us back to Siberia."

They all began laughing at me. "You are too suspicious and too nervous because of the war, and you see everything dark and sinister," they said.

"You really are too stupid, all of you," I cried. "There is a German saying, 'certain stupidity has to be punished' and you will be punished! But why should I suffer with you?"

Why indeed! But there was nothing I could do about it; and no sooner had that stupid fellow said yes to the commandant, the door to our room was locked and a notice put up on the outside of the door, saying, that the group were being taken care of and that no one was to enter. When the Red Cross arrived and read the notice, they 'washed their hands' of us and, once again, we were on our own.

The next day, the buss came and we were herded on to it, taken back to Poland and placed in a jail. It was a certainty, that from that jail, they would have sent us to wherever it was that those who tried to escape were taken.

But it was after the war and with chaos everywhere, everything was make do, including the jails for dissidents; and that, so called jail that we were placed in, was nothing more than an old building that was being used for such purposes.

The intention was to keep us there for a day or two before we were transported to Siberia, or wherever they decided to send us, and they put a Polish policeman inside the room to take care of the group during our stay. He was a pleasant enough fellow, late forties, early fifties, tall and thin with stooped shoulders, and a deeply lined face that looked more like the face e of a craggy cliff.

It was becoming obvious, to them, that I was the only one who really understood what was going on, but it was too late. However, as luck would have it, there was one young man, Pieta, who had been in the Russian army and had learned a few tricks of his own on how to look after himself against the shrewd Russian soldiers, and he asked, "Does anyone here have a watch?"

There were quite a few, and they gave them to him. "Now!" he said, "We have to have a plan; we have to get this Pole on our side."

He spoke a good Polish and he called to him and, speaking with him in a friendly manner, like you might to a close relative, they began laughing and sharing jokes with one another. "You know what, brother, how can we stay here without vodka? It's impossible, Vodka makes the life bearable," he said.

"Jah! Jah! You are right," replied our jailor. "But how can I afford Vodka with what they pay me!"

"No problem," said Pieta, "We have some watches. Why don't you take them to sell and buy enough Vodka for all of us, so that we can enjoy the rest of our stay here?"

The guard was swift to agree; he wanted the money and he wanted Vodka, and here was his chance. So he took the watches and soon returned with plenty of booze.

"Wonderful, wonderful, "said Pieta, "Because of you we have the Vodka; but why should we drink alone? You have been such a good friend, so let us drink together."

The guard's lined face lifted, the grooves almost disappearing; he was very pleased, "Jah, jah! Let's drink together," he laughed.

And so began the party, but whilst he poured mug after mug down his throat - there were no glasses – we only made believe in keeping him company, filling his cup as quickly as it became empty until he fell to the ground in a drunken stupor, and slept the motionless sleep of the dead without thought or feeling.

There was an undercurrent of excitement laced with fear as we watched Pieta grab the rope that had been discovered in a corner cupboard of the room, and begin to tie the man up.

"Someone help me!" he called.

Immediately, everyone sprang to life, dashing here and there in a frenzy of activity whilst one of the young men helped to secure the knots and another turned him over. The guard was snoring away, oblivious to what was going on. They needed a crucial couple of hours before he was found or came to himself, and we all helped to drag his 'dead-weight' body to a far corner of the room, removing his boots and pants and hiding them in the same cupboard in which the rope was found. Then, anxiously, we waited for direction from Moniek who had taken over the leadership of the group.

This was our third attempt to escape and we all knew it would be our last if we didn't succeed; so the stakes were high and we were heady and breathless with a certain amount of expectation and a lot of hope.

We had to be careful not to attract too much attention when we escaped the building where we were detained, and so, two by two, we vacated the premises and caught up with each other on the outskirts of the town, and from there, we ran, keeping a close watch up and down the roads as we went.

By the time the Russians found out that we were gone, we were in Warsaw and in the hands of a Jewish committee, who smuggled us out, using the, least travelled, back roads, avoiding villages and open fields on our journey to West Berlin. While exhausted, more from tension than the journey, our spirits were high with hope and the promise of a normal life at long last.

When we arrived in Berlin, a committee from the 'joint' had gathered there to greet us and, after a long hard look at each one of us in turn, the spokesman said, "We have never met anyone like this before, but we had to see what you people looked like, that were part of the most stupid group we had ever helped to escape into West Germany! First a typical Russian goes out on deck when we made it clear that this was not to happen, and you were all discovered; next some idiot goes to the commandant and falls for his lies. And so we wanted to take a look at you and see for ourselves what kind of fools we were dealing with."

If we hadn't been so relieved, we might have been embarrassed; but we were free at last, and that was all that mattered to us; so we just stood there, listening, with not even one bent head in humiliation.

From West Berlin we were taken to a D.P. camp, for Jewish displaced persons, in Leibheim, that was not far from Munich. There were many such camps that, originally, were for the German soldiers before the war. But now they were transformed by the Americans for the Jewish people until we found places for ourselves, all over the world, and there we were looked after by the Jewish federation or the `joint' as they were commonly called.

While there, I understood that the Jews of Palestine, who were there from before the war, could be contacted to let us know if any of our relatives survived in Eastern Europe. I had two cousins there and hoped that if I got in touch with them, they might be able to tell me who else survived the war. So I went to the 'joint' and gave them the names of my two cousins who lived somewhere in Tel -Aviv.

Sure enough, two weeks later there came a letter giving me the names of two cousins who had survived Auschwitz, and that they were living in a small town near Hanover and Bergen-Belsen where there had, once, been a concentration camp.

Immediately, I contacted them and soon after, I received a letter, telling me that there was no need for me to be alone when I had family to be with. Being older than I, they were married, and they and their husbands insisted that I join them in either one of their homes for as long as I liked. And so I left the camp and went to stay with them.

Before the war, one of my cousins earned a diploma from a business college in Danzig. Aware of this and that she was very good at office work, as well, spoke perfect German, the people in charge of repatriating the Jews, asked her to preside over the Jewish community in the city, which entailed seeing that they had all the necessary food and clothing they needed, after returning from the concentration camps, or wherever it was that they were in hiding from the Germans, and she readily agreed to it.

One day, a doctor Landau walked into her office, seeking clothes and food for himself and his wife, Rae. My cousin, gave him a long hard look, and said, "Doctor Landau, for eight months now, you have been walking past this office, but never thought to step inside to say hello. All of a sudden you come in. I do not want to insult you by calling you a liar, but you look nothing like a Jew; with your blond hair and blue eyes, you look a typical Pole... But I'll tell you what, you go to Bergen-Belson to see a rabbi, and if you can prove to him that you are Jewish, return with his confirmation and you will get whatever is due to you and your wife."

And so he left for Bergen-Belson and returned with the testament to his faith and received the parcels, sent over by the Americans, and that were so important to people like himself, who were striving to get by, after the war, without the daily necessities of life.

There were ten German Jewish families living in that small town, after the war, and about ten Polish Jews and this small congregation decided that an evening together would be in order so that they could get to know each other better, and Dr. Landau and his wife were invited.

It was one of the first parties, after the war, and we laughed and ate together, and listened to each others stories of survival.

I, who was sitting next to Dr. Landau and his wife, asked, "Dr. Landau, how did you manage to survive?"

His eyes turned inward, as though they were looking back into the past. For a moment he didn't speak, and then, suddenly, he wet his bottom lip with his tongue and began. "I realized, right at the beginning of the war, that my wife and I would have no chance of surviving as Jews unless we had false papers to say that we were Poles. But I also knew that we could not survive amongst the Poles because the Poles, one way or another, would find out that we were Jewish, and give us away to the Germans. So where better to hide, than amongst the enemy; because I also knew that amongst the Germans, who could never tell the difference between a Jew and a Pole, it would be easier to survive.

"So, heart in mouth, I went to the German authorities and told them that I am a doctor and would like to go to Germany to practice my profession in one of their hospitals. They were in need of doctors and agreed to my proposal, and there we stayed until the last few weeks of the war when they found out about us."

I could see how he managed to get away with it. He was very blond and blue eyed with a small turned up nose and spoke Polish without a trace of a Jewish accent. I also discovered that he came from a much assimilated family where Yiddish was never spoken, in fact, his whole bearing was that of an upper crust Pole, and his wife came from a similar background to his.

He continued, "Once we knew that we had permission to go to Germany where I would be working as a doctor, my wife taught herself how to pray like a catholic so that when we went to church, there would be no suspicion that we were not whom we said we were.

"Well, I worked in that hospital for two years without fear of being found out. Unfortunately, one day they brought in two Polish doctors to work with us in the hospital; that is when I was in fear of our lives, and I said to my wife, now we are in danger. 'Don't be silly,' she replied, 'no one can possibly suspect that we are Jewish; even we have almost forgotten who we are it has been so long.' Nevertheless, I no longer felt comfortable with the situation.

"I was a surgeon, and they sent in the two Polish doctors to assist me during an operation. I spoke with them in Polish and all appeared to be going well, except, two days later, when my wife and I were at home in the evening, we heard Yiddish songs being sung outside our window and my heart fell. They have us! I said to my wife, and not long after the Gestapo arrived to arrest us and put us in prison.

"But fortune was still on our side. It was only a week before the end of the war, and the Germans were too busy trying to save their own skins to pay too much attention to us. And so they just left us there, and when the Americans came, we were liberated.

"But it wasn't the end of the torment, it bothered me; I needed to know how they found out that I was Jewish. Who told them? What did we do to give ourselves away? And, night and day, I was consumed by such thoughts.

"One day, I was out walking, when I ran into a colleague I worked with at the hospital during the war. He was quite friendly and so I asked him, who was it that gave me away? 'One of the Polish doctors,' he said, 'I certainly didn't know that you were Jewish.'

"So I figured, that being doctors, those two Poles would be working in one of the displaced camps for Polish citizens, and that's what I had to do to get rid of this gnawing inside me, find them! So I went from camp to camp, until I did.

"The moment they saw me, they got ready to stand up to me, believing I was there to hurt them as they hurt me and my wife. Seeing how hostile they were becoming, I said, 'look, relax, the war is over, I didn't come here to take revenge, I came here for one purpose only, I want to know how you knew that I was Jewish?' They exchanged glances, and then, hesitantly, one of them said, 'even under surgery, you had such sad eyes, and this we called, 'the Jewish sad eyes' and that's how we found our Jews, by simply looking into their eyes, and that is how we knew that you were a Jew, otherwise, we would never have guessed'… And knowing gave me the relief I was searching for."

Sad eyes! I mused with a sigh, and a lump formed in my throat when I recalled the look in my father's eyes, eyes that had once sparkled with the joy of living and that, suddenly, became dull with despair. If only he could see me now, sitting here, amongst family, and amidst one of those little pockets of Jews that he explained to me that, somehow, would manage to survive the storm. A fluke of nature, he had said, a fluke of nature.

I stayed with my cousins for six months, and although it was wonderful to be with them, it was a small German city with no young people and nothing there to satisfy my needs. I wanted to do something with my life, even though, at the time, I didn't know exactly what.

The Jews had established an organization called 'ORT' which helped young people to learn a profession of their choice. In my case, it was the nursing profession; and to be able to do this, we were provided with food and lodging whilst in training, for one year.

They sent me to Augsburg in Bavaria to a hospital where there was a D.P. camp for Jews, where a Doctor Osterveil, that was chief of staff over-saw the teaching of the girls who wished to learn the nursing profession, and there I remained for the duration of my training. But, because I was born in Germany, and received my papers from Berlin, I didn't have to live in the hospital like most of the others; I was given, by the German authority, my own apartment, which was about two miles from the hospital and from which I walked back and forth each day.

I found that nursing was far removed from the glamorous profession that the recruiting staff made it out to be. It was all bed pans, blanket washes, scrubbing baths, and trying to deal with one complaining patients after another; and then, after a hard days work, studying well into the night to be able to get through the exams with good grades

While I was there, Dr. Osterveil had a car accident and was very ill with concussion. Still, he managed to remain in charge of his senses. There were eleven Jewish girls who were being taught nursing by him and another, elderly, Jewish doctor. While lying in the hospital bed, unable to move, he called the eleven of us to his side and told us that we had to take turns to sit by him for as long as he remained in hospital. Whether he had become paranoid or not, he was afraid that the doctor looking after him might give him the wrong medication and kill him. We did as he asked, and eventually he recovered and we were able to resume our studies fully and return to our usual duties.

It was exhausting, but I made it through, and at the end of my training, received that precious piece of paper from Doctor Osterveil that said I was qualified.

I was lucky to be very much like my father, who was good at everything he attempted to do. I also had a lot of pride in myself, and studied hard to achieve that nurse's diploma; not that I really considered myself a fully qualified nurse. By today's standards, a year's training would only produce a nurse's aide; but it was a profession worth having, back in those days, when there was a great shortage of hospital staff.

Armed with my certificate of nursing from the ORT organization, I decided to go to Munich where there was a Jewish hospital. Whilst walking along the street, I suddenly heard my name being called. Somewhat surprised, I turned to see who it was, and there was Magda, running along the street towards me. We hadn't seen each other since we were in the Russian gulag together, after which we were dispersed all over Russia, and we, immediately, they fell into each other's arms. "What are you doing here?" she asked with unconcealed delight.

When I explained everything to her, Magda asked if I had somewhere to stay. "I have only just arrived and I am looking for accommodation, something that I can afford." I replied.

Magda was a married woman and older than I. I had always liked her, and looked upon her as an older sister, back in the gulag. So when she said, "Look, you are not going to stay in some cheap hotel, I am very rich, my husband does big business, and we live in a very large apartment, and I am going to take you home with me and you can stay with us until you get married."

I expected nothing less, from that woman. No matter how down she was, in the gulag, she always had a good word for everyone, and tried to do the best she could for them; so I was only too happy to accept her offer.

Indeed, it was a very large apartment, and beautifully appointed with huge double doors to the rooms and molded cornices around the edges of the ceilings. The moment we entered her bedroom, Magda threw open the wardrobe doors and pulled out the drawers, saying, "You can see how many lovely clothes I have, so take whatever you want, pick something nice, because tonight we are going to a Jewish cabaret where all the survivors meet, and there is food, music and dancing, and you are going with us. And as far as going to work, take a few days rest first, you need it, and whenever you are ready, believe me, they will take you."

Magda, the clothes, the apartment, took my breath away. It was like a fairy tale come true, and as soon as I was left alone in the room, I ran my fingers over the fine materials of the clothes with such pleasure; silks, satins and the latest taffetas that I had only heard about but never seen.

I chose a dress of green satin and held it up against myself, and, looking in the mirror, I noticed how it brought out the colour of my eyes and I couldn't' wait to put it on in the evening. I had never worn such a dress; I had never worn any kind of cocktail dress, as they were called. Before the war I was too young, and of course, during the war…!

My thoughts went back to my early days, as a child, and lived in Germany. My mother would wear the most lovely clothes whenever she went out, and that memory took me back to the night when I had asked her if she could go to the ball, and she had replied, 'you are going to a ball, it's called the feather ball,' and she tucked me in and kissed me goodnight… I had to stop myself from thinking back any further or I would have broken down and sobbed my heart out.

I then went in search of the bathroom; a bathroom…such a luxury…! Magda had already put some fresh towels out for me, and I washed, put on the beautiful dress, and arranged my hair in the fashion of the day that I noticed my friend wearing.

Magda wasn't a beautiful woman, but had a warm personality and a friendly manner that made her pleasing to be with; and when she came to fetch me, she looked beautiful in a dress of black velvet that made her skin glow. In return, Magda stared at me in surprise. The green dress fit me as though it had been made for me and enhanced the womanly curves of my figure.

"You look so beautiful...!" she cried. "Just look at you! Look at your eyes... ! Oh! I can't wait to introduce you to all my friends."

Magda's husband smiled at her. He was a nice man, and I couldn't help thinking how fortunate I was to be with them again, and under such different circumstances...Unbelievable!

And so, somewhat self conscious with the new me, I went with them to the cabaret. They already had many married friends, and I was the only single person sitting at the table with them.

Close by, there was another table with a number of couples and one single man. I couldn't help noticing that he was constantly looking at me as though unable to take his eyes off me; but his looks were not particularly to my taste, not that I really knew what my taste was.

Later, when we returned home to the apartment, Magda spoke to me like a sister might. "You know, Margot... don't be mad at me, but then again, you have nothing to lose... there was a gentleman there, this evening, who is well known in the community as a very fine man and a very prosperous person, and some of the friends that he was with, came over, just before we left, and said he would like to meet you and asked if it was possible. Knowing of him and his good reputation, I said yes. So he will be coming to take you out."

I heaved a sigh of disappointment, "Look, Magda, I know who you mean and I am not attracted to this man," I said.

"Okay!" she replied with a shrug, "you don't care for him, so you go out and you come back; but I wouldn't have said yes if I didn't think highly of him, but it is your decision."

What choice did I have? So the gentleman came, and he took me out very nicely, but I felt bound to make it clear to him, and as soon as the evening was over, I said, "I had a very nice time, thank you, but I'm afraid you are not exactly my type, so I think we shouldn't see each other again."

He raised his eye brows… "Let me be equally frank with you," he said, "I am a nice man, and you need to get to know me a little bit more before you make your mind up; and then, when you know me better, if you say to me, you are not my type… well what can I do? Nothing! I cannot force anybody. But I am sure that you will like me. So I will come to pick you up again, and little by little, give me and yourself a chance?"

He didn't beg, he had too much self- assurance for that; he had simply stated the facts as he saw them and I liked that about him, it showed strength of character; so I agreed and we began seeing each other regularly.

David was no pushover, but he knew what he wanted, and he wanted me and treated me very well, but never too well so that I felt his attention overpowering; and little by little, just as he predicted, I got to like him more and more; and eventually, quite a lot more. I began to realize that he was a man I could rely on, and I sorely needed someone like that in my life. As well, his style of living was to my liking, after years of deprivation, it was a welcome relief. It also suited my personality, which was outgoing, just like my father's.

We had been seeing each other for a month. Time was precious, in those days, and a month in our lives might have been a year, and one day, he said to me, "Look, we have been together now, for some time. I have two apartments, one that I live in, the other where I keep my merchandise. How would you like to have a place of your own? You can live in one of my apartments, no strings attached!"

I had got to know him well enough to understand that he meant it, nevertheless I was somewhat uneasy with the idea. "…

You know, you already buy me clothes, you buy me all sorts of things, you are always giving me so much and, I don't want to feel obliged to you, I wouldn't enjoy feeling that way; and then, after all that, I would say no to you, and I would feel bad. I don't think I can accept your offer, but thank you all the same; I really do appreciate the thought!"

He wouldn't let it go there and said "Look, what you call giving, is my pleasure, and you are not beholden to me. If things don't work out, according to your way of thinking, then I will simply say to myself, so what! I gave a Jewish girl who survived the holocaust a good time, so what's the big deal?"

I couldn't deny that it was tempting and stared at him for a while before making up my mind; and then – "In that case… I wall take the apartment!" I said. And thus began a new phase in my life.

We both knew what it was to suffer the loss of a family, and in this we were one; but more importantly, not only did we got on well together but were in tune with one another. So what could have been more natural than to spend the rest of our days together?

David.

David was the first of five children born to his parents. They were a poor, very religious family, and when David finished Cheider (Jewish elementary) and the public elementary school, that he attended, he had to go out and do business to help feed his family who were, practically, on the edge of, day to day, hunger.

Poland wasn't an easy country to do business in, especially if you were poor, and David, my husband, would go out into the countryside, where the peasants had their farms, and he would buy and sell whatever he could lay his hands on.

Indeed, he was a born businessman, with a mathematical brain, that would have defied the modern day computer, and with all that of an uneducated country boy, in no time, he was doing well, so well, that in two years, he was able to buy his parents a farm where they kept geese for the feathers, and sufficient employees to pluck the geese for their down to sell in the big cities where the manufacturers filled their, billowing, eiderdowns and pillows with the much needed, light as air, feathers. Meanwhile, he would go out buying eggs, butter cheese, and transport them to cities such as Krakow, Lodz and Warsaw; and his business went from success to success.

In the course of doing all this, my husband met a man who owned a large transport company who had taken a liking to him; and the man came to him, one day, and said, "You know, you are just the right person for my daughter." And he invited David to meet her.

They liked each other immediately, and after they were married, David was made a co-owner of the transport Company and eventually, owned a small, private, Fiat car of his own which, in itself, was really something, back in those days, for someone from his, poor, background.

They set up house in the town of Novykorczyn when all at once they were faced with war, sending the entire Jewish population into a flurry of anxiety. They had survived anti-Semitism, sometimes at its extreme, over the years; but nothing as extreme as what was now going on since Hitler's conquest of Eastern Europe; and it was frightening.

When the war began, and it became obvious that the Germans would soon occupy Poland, those who were able, exchanged their currency for small denominations of that world currency, gold, in readiness to flee should the time come.

They waited too long, as so many do when faced with leaving their home and country behind. The year was 1942 and overnight it happened, leaving them horrified and in a state of shock, with no chance to flee, when, jack booted and bellowing orders, members of that terrifying gang of vicious, supposedly, human beings broke down doors and entered homes shouting, arouse, arouse in their guttural tongue, manhandling the occupants with no thought to age or gender and, literally, throwing them out into the street.

My husband and his first wife, with daughter in arms, watched, terrified, from behind a chink in the curtains, knowing that they, as well, would soon be going through the same experience. Suddenly, his wife turned to him and said, "You must go up into the attic and hide yourself; you have to survive."

"What are you saying? We will all go up into the attic, if we are to survive, we will survive together," he said.

"That would be impossible," she replied. "the baby will cry and they would find us and we will all suffer the same fate. No! You must live so that we will be remembered and you will bear witness to everything you see here today. If you survive, you will tell this story."

His heart filled with pain, he could not contemplate such a thing, and argued with her; but she was insistent and with time no longer on their side, the decision had to be made swiftly. He realized that she was right; no matter what his feelings were, someone had to survive and sad as it was, God willing, he would do his best to survive, for her and for their child's sake; and so it was decided.

How do you say goodbye to loved ones you knew you would never see again? There are no words, only the soundless feeling of a heart shattering into tiny pieces of despair; and so, with one last, lingering, look, he swallowed his tears, turned away, and then, with leaden steps, and eyes misted by the pain he had to bear, he mounted the stairs to the attic and chose a corner from where he would be able to watch, from a small window as, with the child clinging to her, his wife was taken away. What took place next knocked the breath out of him.

The Gestapo had rounded up all the Jews of the town, his parents, two brothers and a sister with her husband amongst them; and as they stood there, with the others, in the centre of the street, looking like a flock of lost sheep while waiting to be told what to do, the German soldiers, without any warning, opened fire, mowing them down as if they were nothing more than weeds in the cracks of the stones that needed to be got rid of.

Turned to ice, he froze to the spot. He wanted to scream, but not a sound left his lips. Terror gripped his whole inside, and as he thawed, he began shaking. - He should have been with them. He should have been with them- Was all he could think about; but now it was too late.

He sank to the floor; he had no wish to see them being disposed of in any way, as disposed of he knew they had to be. The German's were not about to leave any evidence of their savagery even though they thought themselves to be in the right. A fact, they believed history would prove.

To perform such an atrocity needs hearts of steel, and you have to wonder in what dread furnace were such hearts forged

Slowly, as he came to himself, he realized that it was a miracle that they had overlooked the attic. Probably, he thought, that when they saw his wife and child downstairs, they assumed if anyone was in hiding, they would have taken them with them.

How long he sat there on the floor, trying to make sense of it all, he had no idea, but all at once, it was dark. Still shaken, unsteadily, he rose to his feet and looked down into the street. There was no moon, no stars, only the pitch black of the night sky. He had to get out of there, out of the town; into the country, perhaps? He was still too distressed, his head too muddled; but he knew he couldn't stay where he was forever. And so, in the still of the night, when everyone else in the town must have been shuttered away from the events that took place in the daytime, he made his way down the stairs and out onto the street, uncertain which way to turn.

It so happened, that there were three others, two men and a girl, who escaped detection in the same manner; and as my husband walked, stealthily, along the street, close to the wall for cover as he went, to his surprise, he met up with them. They too, were looking to escape the town.

"So where are you going?" asked David.

"To a farm not too far away," replied Saul, one of the men.

"How come?"

"Well, you see it's like this. The farmer, a poor but very religious man, knew my father and a few month ago, when he realized things had not been going well for the Jews for years, he came to see us and told us of a dream he had where an angel visited him and told him that if he saved some Jews, then he would most surely go to heaven and he wanted to go to heaven; therefore, he said, should the time come when you are in need of shelter, me and my wife will give it to you."

"But can you trust him? The Germans play roughly with those who would defy them."

"What alternative do we have? Anyhow we cannot be worse off than we are now."

And so, hiding in the shadows, they made their way into the countryside and on to the lowly farmer's humble dwelling. When the farmer answered the soft knocking on his door and saw the four Jews standing there, looking from left to right, to make sure they weren't followed, he was only too happy to take them into the warmth where his wife poured each of them a comforting cup of lemon tea.

It was a tiny cottage with only a kitchen, which also served as a living room, and one bedroom. Anyhow, a place to hide them had to be found that would leave them completely out of sight and the barn, which stood well away from the cottage, was chosen. Fortunately, the farm's closest neighbour was well over a mile away, which helped to make them secluded from prying eyes. And so, under cover of darkness, they burrowed beneath the dirt floor of the barn, digging a large enough hole to house all four of them in the pit and just enough room to put together stacked bunks of rough wood either side. As for privacy, there was no such thing, even for the girl; it was war and there was no place for modesty. And there they remained for the duration of the war, with enough blankets and food to make it as comfortable as possible. Not that it was that comfortable, there was little air, and the farmer would open the barn door just a mite, at night, so that they could come up out of their hole and breathe a little fresh air before returning to the dark and damp interior of the shelter.

Still the farmer was uneasy. As mentioned, he was a religious man who went to church and confession every week without fail, and he was terrified of the priest and what he would do if he were to confess that he was harbouring four Jews, knowing full well that he would tell him, in no uncertain way, to give them up to the Nazis. To him, it was a great dilemma; he didn't want to fall foul of the priest whom he feared and he dearly wanted to go to heaven; and so he approached the four with his problem.

It was troubling for them and they gave it much thought until Paul came up with a solution. "You used to be in the coal mines, "he said, "but you left because you got the lung disease silicosis from the coal dust. What you must do is this. Tell your wife to go to the priest and tell him that your condition is getting worse and then see what he has to say.

Just as the four hoped he would, upon hearing this, the priest not only worried about his congregation but about himself as well, and after blessing her for having come forward with their situation, he said a prayer blessing them both and told the farmer's wife that they must keep away from the church and the community for as long as necessary.

That was not the end of the problem. The four realized that the famer was becoming restless. He was cut off from his religion and missed his old way of life; he was also scared to wander too far away from the farm and missed the social atmosphere of the church; realizing this, the boys needed to come up with a plan to keep him from becoming depressed.

"Cards! Does anyone happen to have a pack of cards?" asked one of them.

They looked at each other in dismay, and shook their heads.

"Perhaps the farmer has a pack. Let us find out."

It so happened the farmer's wife recalled seeing a pack of cards hidden in an old shoe box many years ago and she and her husband set out to search for it and found it amongst a number of boxes they planned to throw out, but, somehow, never got around to it; And there amongst a lot of junk inside the shoe box, was a worn pack of cards, the king, face up, on top. A good omen, thought the superstitious farmer, and immediately ran to the dugout, and with a broad smile, handed them over to his 'guests'.

The plan was to teach the farmer a game that four could play, and let him win every time. They knew how a person could get hooked on such games, and they made certain of his commitment, by giving him a small gold coin, after each game, from the cash of gold each of them managed to take with them when they escaped the Germans, explaining to him that it was his reward for being so good at the game.

Gambling most certainly could become a disease and one that the farmer was not immune to; and every day he would visit them with anticipation and the eagerness of the gambler who was on a winning streak.

The farm wasn't yielding enough to eat for any of them; and not only were the four fugitives hungry, but the farmer and his wife as well; and so, when the farmer arrived for his daily game of cards, before he left, they said to him, "We will give you a small amount of gold each week so that your wife can go into town to buy enough provisions to feed us all for that week."

The farmer's eyes lit up. The thought of filling his belly with meat, once again, was to his liking and he readily agreed.

"But!" They warned, "She must be careful not to attract attention; If she spends too much they will get suspicious and report to the police and then, not only will we be caught, but, in all probability, you and your wife will be sent to prison for keeping us hidden."

The farmer agreed. "I will speak to my wife," he said. "We want to eat but we don't want to be caught." He swallowed. "I will tell my wife what you told me. She will do as you say. She will tell the store keeper she robbed a Jew."

And so they ate enough to stave off hunger, slept as much as they were able on the rough hewn planks of wood the bunks were made from; sweated some in summer and shivered in winter until the day arrived when the farmer came rushing in to their hole in the ground announcing with excitement

"It's over. The war is over; the Germans have lost. You are free! Free!" And laughing for joy, he threw his arms up in the air, turned his face heavenward and cried, "Thank you Lord, thank you."

The farmer, unable to read and with no radio, the four fugitives had no access to information save for the gossip the farmer's wife brought home about the advancing allied forces across Europe, from the storekeeper where she bought the weekly rations.

Having lived a long time, now, with the threat of being captured hanging over their heads, they took the news warily. Who knew what some rogue German officers might do when faced with capture; so it took a while before they felt secure enough to venture out into the sunshine and when they eventually did, with the sun blinding them, after living so long with nothing but a small oil lamp for light, it was a breathtaking, glorious moment. They wanted to run and hop, skip and jump. The warm, May, air as it touched the skin of the face felt like the caress of a gentle hand. The scent of the earth intoxicated their senses; and the sight of the trees in full leaf made them shed tears of joy. They had not dared to hope for fear of disappointment. Now there was no need to long for hope, hope was theirs; it belonged to them once again.

Before they left their hiding place behind, they gave the farmer and his wife a handsome gift of gold coins. He had saved their lives and deserved as much; and then each of them left to go their own way.

My husband, in his naivety, ventured back into his home town, believing he might find some of their prized possessions, no matter how small, that may still be in their hiding place in the attic of their house.

Fortunately, before he reached his door, he was spotted by an old Polish woman that recognised him. In haste, she approached him and with a glance to left and right, whispered, "Quick, quick, run away. There are men, in the town, who are watching and waiting for Jews, such as you, who come back to find whatever they had left behind, and they will kill you." (Many were killed by such men. One of the tragedies of war and its aftermath.)

My husband didn't need to be told twice, and fearful for his life he immediately left for the large and lovely city of Krakow where he found a suitable apartment for himself.

When he was well settled in, he got in touch with the farmer and invited him to visit him. The farmer had never been to the big city and my husband wished to give this good man a nice time as an extra thank you for what he had done for him. Indeed, the farmer had never been inside anything more than the like of his humble cottage and was only too glad to accept the offer.

The biggest surprise of all came when he asked where he could relieve himself and my husband showed him the bath room that boasted a toilet as well as a hand basin and bath.

His eyes widened in horror, "You want me to do it in there!" he cried.

"Of course!" declared my husband.

He couldn't believe his ears and said, "I didn't know that people in the city are such pigs, and that they would do such things inside the home they lived."

My husband smiled. This good man had saved his life, and not wanting to make him feel small, he said, as you might to an innocent child, "Yes, this is life in the big city. Not as good and clean as life in the countryside."

Despite his feelings, and shaking his head in disbelief, the farmer couldn't help but use the facility.

It was shortly after that that my husband concluded that Poland was no longer for him and decided on Munich, a large German city as far removed from the little town in Poland that he came from. Why Munich? Fate is a strange thing. Perhaps, somewhere inside his head, he heard its voice calling to him. He was an entrepreneur by nature and Germany was wide open, after the beating it took at the hands of the allies. It had become a land of opportunity for those with initiative enough to 'take it on'; and my husband was such a person.

I also mentioned the word 'fate' for sure enough; it was there, in Munich and only there where he was destined to meet the right woman to be his partner for life.

The gold and jewelry business in Germany was beginning to thrive again; and when walking along one of Munich's busy thoroughfares, my husband stopped in front of a jewellery store window that rather took his fancy, and being of a positive nature, immediately entered the establishment and introduced himself to the owner. "I am a Jew from Poland and I am a business man, and would like to buy and sell jewellery".

The owner smiled, he was immediately taken by the manner of the young man, and said "As it happens you have come on the right day. I have just opened the store after a long absence; you see, this respected and well established business had been in my family for generations before the war, and one day, the Nazis, who were in power then, came to my store and said that I should join the party as an example to others. I explained that I wasn't interested in politics. It upset them, and they said that if I didn't join, they would close the store down, and despite all my pleas, that is what they did. They took my business, without any provocation at all and shut it down, just like that!

"Angry and frustrated, I took whatever I needed to survive and went deep into the forest and there I lived out the war chopping wood. Me! A jeweller, chopping wood; but that is all I wanted to do after being treated in such a way by the Hitler regime. Now my friend, as I said, you have come on the right day and to the right person."

Indeed, the right day and the right person it was, and a good relationship was established, one that prospered well for each of them; and with everything going so well, my husband took an apartment, and soon after had to take another to warehouse the volume of goods he had ready for distribution at any given time.

That was the stage in life that he had reached when, out one evening at a restaurant with friends, a young woman, sitting at another table across the room, caught his eye, and instantly, he knew that she was the one he wanted to spend his life with; and set the wheels in motion to meet her.

With no family and just a few select friends in attendance, we went to the office of a Reform rabbi, who performed the ceremony; and standing before him, dressed in our best, we were happily joined together for the rest of our days.

I looked lovely, so I was told. I already had good taste in clothes and drew the admiration of all present, especially from my new husband whose eyes shone with pride each time he looked at me. We celebrated the event by booking a table at a good restaurant where a fine feast was laid on for us and our guests. Peace had entered our lives again, and happiness.

Some time later, another, happy, event took place – the birth of our daughter. Imagine my husbands joy. Imagine my joy. We named her Ruth, after my mother.

In 1951, with our daughter just one year old, we crossed the Atlantic to the American continent, and made our home in Montreal, Canada, and never looked back. Our lives were complete.

In the nineteen eighties, Margaret Thatcher, then British prime minister, met with Gorbachov, Her Russian counterpart, and said, afterwards, 'Here is a man we can do business with.' As well, President Reagan was instrumental in demanding Gorbachov to 'Take down the wall'. Not long after, in November 1989, the Wall came down between East and West Berlin.

Two, maybe three months later, I had a strong desire to return to East Berlin, where I had lived with my parents before our escape to Poland. It was a need that couldn't be quietened until I had seen for myself if the apartment building where we lived was still standing – if so, I wanted to see it once again.

I travelled on my own to Berlin, where I booked into an hotel, and then went out and took a taxi to that part of the city that once had been behind the wall.

When the taxi driver heard that I wanted to go to East Berlin, he said, "Look, I'm a young fellow and was born after the war. I have no idea where anything is in that part of the city."

"But you are a taxi driver, a German guy," said I "You must have a map of the whole city?"

"Yes, yes, you are right," he laughed, "and took out the map.

"Look," I said, "find Alexander Platz. Where I want to go is a street off Alexander Platz. Now, when we get there, we will ask around and, maybe, someone will be able to direct us to Weinmeister Strasse

When we came to Alexander Platz, nothing was as I remembered it. The big square that used to stand in the centre of the street was now divided into small pieces which were surrounded by mound after mound of broken bricks, smashed concrete and mangled masonry. Neither were there any people on the street to ask for directions. It was like a ghost town that had been torn to pieces with nowhere for anyone to go. Still, we didn't give up and continued the search for someone, anyone who might help us.

At last we came across someone who was able to direct us to Weinmeister Strasse, or what was left of it. I didn't know what to expect, but certainly not what confronted me. Everything had been dynamited, leaving nothing but rubble for the rats of the city to hide in. Holding my breath, as I looked around, trying to find something of that remembered past, my eyes caught site of a sign that read, No. 4. And immediately, I cried out with excitement, "This is it! This is where I lived; and pointed to the only building that was still standing in the midst of all the demolished sites that were now nothing but derelict heaps of rubbish.

The building was cordoned off, obviously ready for the same fate as everything else in that part of the city; and still with excitement, I explained to the taxi driver my reason for coming to Berlin, to see the place where I lived before the war; and he then understood that I was a Jewish survivor of the war.

Himself, somewhat excited, he said to me, "Please, remain in the taxi; I will go and find someone in authority, who will let you inside the building." And off he went and found the engineer who was getting ready to demolish the building, and he explained to him that he had a woman in the car, who lived there, in the building, before the war, and that she wanted to go inside to look around.

The engineer was beside himself with joy, when he heard, and running over to the taxi, cried, "This is wonderful, wonderful. It's a story that I will tell my grandchildren, over and over, that a woman came all the way from the American continent, to see the place where she lived, a long time ago, before the war, and arrived just one half hour before it was due to be torn down. So please, madam, come with me and it will be my pleasure to take you inside. But, I must tell you, there is not much left to see."

So I stepped out of the taxi and went with the engineer, eager to see for myself what was left of the inside of the building.

There was little to see, indeed. The staircase was still there, but all that was left of the apartments was a skeleton of what had been. And I stood there, staring, overwhelmed by grief, and my brain, shut down, not wishing to recall those times so long ago, for to remember, would have been too much for me to bear.

I remained in Berlin for another few days, then returned to Montreal, grateful to be with my family, once again.

It was 1959, and my husband and I, who were living in Montreal, were invited to an evening at a friend's house, where I was introduced to a man who, when I asked the burning question, that every survivor asks another survivor, where were you from? He replied that he was from Wloclawek, in Poland; and I told him that I went to school there, and that I had two cousins that had lived there, Izio and Yulak. Immediately, he inquired, "How is your cousin Izio?"

"My cousin Izio is dead," I replied.

"No he isn't; he is living in Israel," he said

I couldn't believe my ears. "Where in Israel?" I asked in exited confusion.

So the man said to me "Write to the authorities in Tel-Aviv and they will put you in touch with the Jewish agency that will have information about your cousin." And he gave me the address of the organization from Wloclawek that worked in Tel-Aviv.

Filled with expectation as well as absolute joy, I wrote to the organization in Tel-Aviv, asking them to let me know of the whereabouts of my cousin Izio Szkolnik, and shortly afterwards, I received a letter from him himself. Eager to see Izio, once again, I Immediately made arrangements to go to Israel, taking my daughter with me, to see him and other members of my family, on my father's side, that had survived the war.

The reunion was wonderful, full of pathos, joy and a good deal of heart ache as I listened to their stories of survival.

MY cousin Izio was the first to recount his miraculous escape from the clutches of the Gestapo. "Everyone in the city of Wloclawek knew the Germans were coming, but we were caught by surprise when they arrived as soon as they did. So, while I walked along the street, it seemed to me that, from out of nowhere they came and swooped down on a number of Jews, with me amongst them, and put us all in prison.

"A day later, one of the soldiers entered the prison with the purpose of finding out if there was an electrician amongst us that could do some, necessary, work for him.

"I was a tool maker by trade, but knew quite a bit about electricity, and terrified of what might happen to me otherwise, I stepped forward.

"It didn't take long before the German soldier realized that I was not what I said I was; but for whatever reason, he took me aside and said, "I can see you are no electrician."

"I had no alternative but to tell the truth. "I am a tool maker," I said. "But while I was learning to be a toolmaker, I had to know something about electricity; and since you asked for an electrician, I believed that I could help you out."

My family, including my maternal grandmother, always spoke German at home; so Izio found it easy to converse with the German soldier in German, who then said to him, "Listen, young man, If I send you back to prison, you will face certain death. Now I have a suggestion that you must take very seriously. I will give you money, and then you must run, as fast as you can, to the train station and take a train to Bialystok. There is no border between here and there as yet, and you will be safe because over there you will be free. As well, you have a very good trade that is needed and so you will survive the war. But if you do not listen to me and go to see your mother, who you tell me lives in this city, before you leave, instead of making for the station right away, you will be caught, I will be reprimanded, and it will all have been for nothing. But if you run to the station, even though they will not be pleased with the situation, I will manage to convince them that it wasn't my fault that you ran away. So take the money, don't look back and run as fast as you can to the station."

"And so, I took the money and ran to the station as he said I was to do; and when I reached Bialystok, I registered to work in Russia in Donbas, where they needed tool makers.

"And that is how I survived the war," said Izio, "Working in Donbas as a tool maker."

Now Izio had a brother, Yulac, who was going to high school, where, after six years of study, he gained a certificate of education that was equivalent to a Bachelors degree, at university, and from there, he was supposed to go to Paris to study medicine. That was in June, and the war broke out in September. which made it impossible for him to go to Paris and pursue his dream of becoming a doctor.

Now, he had a friend, at school, Stanislaw Person who studied with him, and who spent more time in Yulac's home than his own, where Yulac lived with his grandmother who went to a German boarding school, when young, where she made friends with many German girls of the Catholic faith; one in particular with whom she remained bosom pals throughout her life, and even when they were old, they continued to meet a few times a week, in the city of Wloclawek, where they lived, and Stanislaw Person was her grandson. Not only were the two women close, but the two families, of different faith, were also as close as if connected by blood.

When the German army entered Wloclawek, they asked Stanislaw's father, who owned a tool factory, to come to the German occupational authorities, that said to him, "You are a German. You are not only well known by the community, but you are well respected, and we want you to be the mayor of this city."

To which he, immediately, replied, "I am very honoured by your proposal and it is true that I am German, but I was born in Poland and I have Polish citizenship, as well, the Poles have always been good to me. How can I be mayor of an occupied city and be put there by occupational forces!"

The very next night, they came to his home, dragged him out into the square, and shot him while his son, Stanislaw, together with his entire family, stood by and watched in horror.

How Stanislaw despised the German soldiers who had done that to his father! How he hated them because of their brutal treatment and persecution of the Jews with whom he had always been close. It was a struggle for him to endure and come to terms with; and out of desperation and anger, he suddenly disappeared and it was learned that he had joined the Polish underground.

Still in Tel Aviv, I met another cousin, a girl named Lilka Tick who told her the story about Stanislaw Person and what happened to him.

"Margot!" she said, "You must have read the book, 'The Wall'. Well, before the uprising of the Warsaw ghetto, there were a few Jewish groups, that were given false Arian Papers as Poles, that were being smuggled out, through the sewers, to the Polish side at night. Now there was a small Polish, underground, cell, that was working together with the Jews and not against them, and whilst I was making my way through the rat infested sewer with other Jews from the ghetto, one that was from the underground and who wasn't a Jew, but would go with us to lead us out, he called to us, is there anyone here that was from the city of Wloclawek?"

"I answered, I went to high school in that city, but I am from Alexandrow."

He then asked, "Did you see or hear anything about Margot Davidowitch?"

"Immediately, I replied, 'I saw her mother in the Warsaw ghetto, and she told me that Margot is in Russia."

"'I am so glad,' he said, and told me that if, after the war, I have survived, I must tell her what Stanislaw Person was doing. I am telling it to you because I know that I am going to be shot. I know that the S.S. are aware of what is going on, and they have my name and are waiting for me and will shoot me as soon as I appear on the other side. Now when I leave the sewer, don't follow in my direction, go the other way, because they are after me and will shoot to kill."

And that is the story she told me about Stanislaw Person, a Polish, German Catholic young man that died doing good for the Jews of the Warsaw ghetto.

A sad silence followed.

Another time, when I went to Israel to see my cousins, I was standing on Ben Yahuda Street in Tel Aviv, when a car passed by, and in that car was Mr. Kay and his driver; and Mr. Kay began shouting "High, Margot, Margot, "and the car stopped and he stepped out and we hugged and kissed and he asked. "What are you doing here, Margot?"

I said, "I am here to see my family. What are you doing here, Mr. Kay?"

And he said, "We are all here living on a Kibbutz. My daughter Sarah married an important man and we have grand children. We do not steal any more. Josh and Mendel work very hard on the Kibbutz, and my wife and I are semi retired, and we are very happy."

And so we hugged again and then said goodbye.

About three years later, I made another of my, subsequent, many trips to Israel, where I spent time with my cousin Izio who told me a heart warming story of what happened when he went back to Poland, with his wife and a friend, to take the waters, physiotherapy and the healing baths at a, once world famous, summer resort and spa, before the war, in the city of Ciechocinek.

VICTIM OF CIRCUMSTANCES

In summer it being overbearingly hot in Israel, Izio decided to take his wife and, together with another couple, from Tel-Aviv, who were also from Wloclawek, before the war, they travelled to Poland and to that particular spa, where the climate was more temperate, and where, for whatever reason, they booked into different hotels.

As with all, reputable, spas, before you are able to take what the facility had to offer, you must go through a rigorous physical examination, by an attending physician, to rule out such as heart problems, diabetes, hypertension, etc. in order to take the baths and whatever treatment would be prescribed in the event that all was well. There was also a diet to be recommended to suit different patient's particular needs

At the hotel, where Izio's friends were staying, an appointment, the following day was made for them, with the doctor. The husband was seen first, and as he entered the surgery, he said in Polish, "good morning Doctor."

The doctor, looked up at him and asked, "From which city in Poland are you originally from?"

"From Wloclawek," he replied.

When the doctor heard this he asked, "Do you know anything about the Szkolniks?"

"Yes!" he said, "he is staying at the other hotel."

The doctor was absolutely stunned, and, overcome with emotion, he said, "Look, I am too shaken to go on with the examination. Would you mind coming back half an hour later?"

Bewildered, the man said, "Of course!"

The doctor then phoned the manager and told him not to send any more patients in to see him, took his jacket off its hanger, and rushed over the other hotel, and asked for Szkolnik, expecting to see his old friend, from school, Yulac.

It was Izio, Yulac's' elder brother that walked towards him. Nevertheless, despite his disappointment, he threw his arms around him and embraced him, although it was yulac who was in his class, at school, but he also knew his brother Izio, and just for a moment, when he saw him, because he had forgotten that his friend had an older brother, he actually thought it was his good friend Yulac.

After the excitement had died down, the Doctor asked Izio, "Yulac?"

Eyes cast down, Izio shook his head.

"Do you know what happened?"

"Yes!" replied Izio. "I do because, after the war I met some people who knew what happened to him.

"...He was engaged to a girl from a very wealthy and prominent family that were smuggled out by an underground cell that was doing this, and they were directed to a farm whose owner, in all probability, told the cell that he would hide the family, but, he had to be paid for doing so.

"It was agreed, and when the family entered the farm house, under the threat of a gun, the farmer made them strip down to their bare skin, took their money, jewellery, whatever they had on them, and then, one by one, shot them," said izio, swallowing with emotion.

It was an emotional moment for both... Then breaking the silence, the doctor said, "You know, I still have a school photo, at home, of the whole class after we finished our degree, and Yulac is on that picture. I will make a copy of it and give it to you."

And so he did, and on that photo was not only Yulac, but Stanislaw Person.

When Izio returned to Tel-Aviv, he made a copy of it for me and I have it to this day, in my apartment in Miami.

VICTIM OF CIRCUMSTANCES

A heartbreaking story, yes, but a story filled with the emotion of a time past and lost forever, except for a photograph that reminds me of a town filled with people whom I loved and remember to this day and who will stay a part of me and my life forever.

Indeed—A time lost and found again in a photograph.

Stanislow Person, young man who saved Jews

About Margot Swicarcik

Margot Swicarcik and her husband, David, immigrated from Germany to Canada, in 1951, where they settled in Montreal Quebec until the death of David, since when, Margot, has been living in Toronto.

This woman, who speaks four languages, and has lost none of her bustling drive, is now in her nineties, and although she enjoys speaking, and has the ability to hold an audiences captive with her riveting presence, she is reluctant to speak of that tragic time, when she lived under the terror of a Europe, at the mercy of the maniac Hitler intent upon the destruction of the Jewish people. And later, in Russia, lived under another maniac, Stalin, who reportedly put more people to death than Hitler, Jews being amongst them.

Margot spends the winter in Miami Florida where she was asked to tell of her life during the war. Apart from this biography, it is the only occasion when she has spoken, to an audience, of the shocking horrors that took place at a time in history like no other.

About Rita Baker

I've been writing since the age of five when I discovered the magic of words. At first, fairy tales, and as I grew so my stories grew with me. Then came poetry. But it was when my children left home and I found time to write my first novel that I felt complete.

I have been greatly influenced by biographical novels and nonfiction works such as The Conspiracy of Fools. I am also a fan of Somerset Maugham and John Grisham—anything that involves lawyers and complex characters. My marriage to a British lawyer also helped me develop a deep insight into the legal profession. This book written for my husband, is a novel about lawyers, the good, the bad, the holy and not so holy. And I enjoyed every minute writing it.

A lawyer is always lurking somewhere in my books. I can never escape them. I don't want to. They have been an integral part of my life—a life filled with everything you could wish for in a marriage filled with love and honour.

As far back as I can remember, there was a nagging that wouldn't let go of me and from the very first book, at the end of the very first page, the nagging left and never returned.

We don' always discover who we are, or who we are meant to be, as in the tragic case of Archie Bingham But when we do, and know where we are heading then that certainty will help us through life's winding paths in a world filled with craggy cliffs and silent plains, to the sparkling rivers that rush to fill the depths of the turbulent seas and oceans.

As Alexander Pope said – Know then thyself, presume not God to scan. The proper study of mankind is man. —And thus it is.

Love, hope, passion. Be it for another, be it for God, what would we do, what would we be without it—nothing, and how much less could we be!

Now I am without my husband, but not his memory. That lives on in all my novels. But that is another story, and one I hope you will discover between the pages of this book.

Live…cast doubt aside, evil and uncertainty. And who knows what you may find…! Or what Archie Bingham might have found.

Made in the USA
Monee, IL
23 February 2020